Other books in the growing Faithgirlz™ library

The Faithgirlz!™ Bible
NIV Faithgirlz!™ Backpack Bible
My Faithgirlz!™ Journal

The Sophie Series

Sophie's World (Book One)
Sophie's Secret (Book Two)
Sophie Under Pressure (Book Three)
Sophie Steps Up (Book Four)
Sophie's First Dance (Book Five)
Sophie's Stormy Summer (Book Six)
Sophie's Friendship Fiasco (Book Seven)
Sophie and the New Girl (Book Eight)
Sophie Flakes Out (Book Nine)
Sophie Loves Jimmy (Book Ten)
Sophie's Drama (Book Eleven)
Sophie Gets Real (Book Twelve)

Nonfiction

No Boys Allowed
Girlz Rock
Chick Chat
Shine On, Girl!
What's a Girl to Do?: Finding Faith in Everyday Life

Check out www.faithgirlz.com

faiThGirLz!

Shine on, Girl!

Devotions to keep you sparkling

Written by Kristi Holl
with Jennifer Vogtlin

zonderkidz

ZONDERVAN.COM/
AUTHORTRACKER

ZONDERKIDZ

Shine On, Girl!
Text copyright „ 2006 by Kristi Holl

Requests for information should be addressed to:

Zonderkidz, Grand Rapids, Michigan 49530

Library of Congress Cataloging-in-Publication Data

Holl, Kristi.
  Shine on, girl! : devotions to keep you sparkling / Kristi Holl ; with Jennifer Vogtlin.
    p. cm. -- (Faithgirlz)
  ISBN 978-0-310-71144-5 (softcover)
    1. Girls--Religious life--Juvenile literature. 2. Devotional calendars--Juvenile literature.
  I. Vogtlin, Jennifer, 1976- II. Title. III. Series.
  BV4551.3.H65 2006
  242'.62--dc22

                                                        2006007565

Art Direction: Merit Alderink
Cover design: Sarah Molegraaf
Illustrated by: Robin Zingone
Interior design: Susan Ambs
Interior composition: Ruth Bandstra

Printed in the United States

09 10 11 12 13 14 15 16 17 18 • 30 29 28 27 26 25 24 23 22 21 20 19 18 17 16 15 14 13 12 11 10 9 8 7 6

Contents

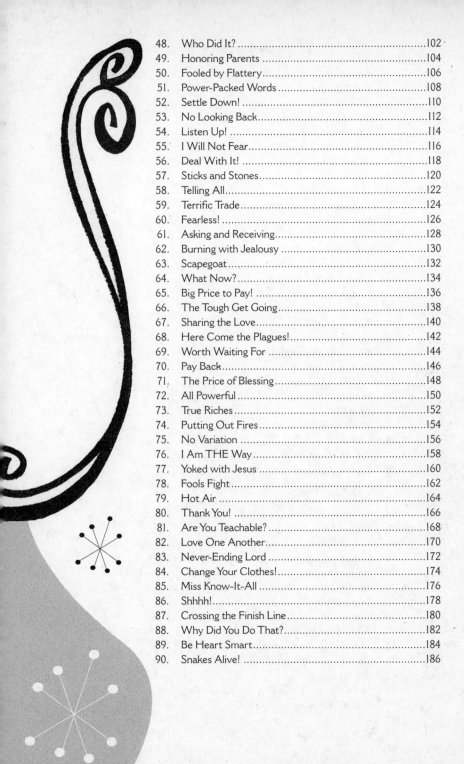

So we fix our eyes not on what is seen, but on what is unseen.
For what is seen is temporary, but what is unseen is eternal.

–2 Corinthians 4:18

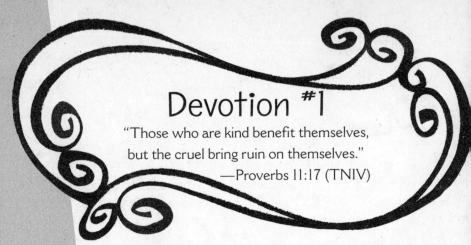

Devotion #1

"Those who are kind benefit themselves,
but the cruel bring ruin on themselves."
—Proverbs 11:17 (TNIV)

Payback

A kind and unselfish person who gives to others is blessed in return. On the other hand, someone who is harsh and insensitive to the suffering of others will be treated the same way.

Amber's grandma had fallen and broken her arm. Grandma loved a clean house, and Amber knew she'd appreciate having someone clean it for her. With her cast, it was too hard for Grandma to drag the vacuum around or scrub out the tub. To be honest, Amber wished she didn't have to spend her Saturday cleaning Grandma's house. However, because she cared, she went anyway. Several hours later, with the house sparkling, Grandma and Amber sat in the porch swing, eating ice cream and laughing about things Amber had done when she was younger. Grandma also shared some stories about her own childhood, things that surprised Amber. By the time Amber had to leave, she hated to go. The joy and laughter far outweighed the energy she'd spent cleaning.

When you give to someone in need—whether it's your money, your time, or your talents—you are planting a seed. If you give just a little, the blessings you get back will be little as well. If you give a lot, the harvest of gratitude, joy, and peace will be huge. "Remember this—a farmer who plants only a few seeds will get a small crop. But the one who plants generously will get a generous crop" (2 Corinthians 9:6 NLT). Be generous—scatter your seed far and wide! Then enjoy your bumper crop of blessings.

Did You Know ...

a simple phone call can get you started giving back to others? Call your pastor or the local Salvation Army to find easy ways to help. "Blessed are the merciful, for they will be shown mercy" (Matthew 5:7 TNIV).

More To Explore: Galatians 6:7

Girl Talk:

When was the last time you served someone just because they needed assistance? Who could use some help from you right now? Make a plan to help them.

God Talk:

Lord, sometimes I get so involved in my life that I forget about others. Help me find ways to give to other people. I want to be a blessing to them and to you. Amen.

Devotion #2

"Unto You, O my Strength, I will sing praises;
for God is my Defense, my Fortress, and High Tower,
the God Who shows me mercy and steadfast love."
—Psalm 59:17 (AMP)

Praise The Lord!

We worship and thank God for many different things. He is our strength when we're weak and our protection when we're attacked. He's our fortress to hide in when we're afraid, our mercy when we make mistakes, and our love when we are lonely. God has so many awesome qualities that deserve praise!

As you sit by the stream, a deep peace flows through you as the water flows downstream. How much you have to be thankful for! You can hardly believe the changes since last year. Your dad's serious illness is over, and he's found an even better job than before. The boy who was picking on you at school has moved away. Your parents have gone to counseling and worked hard, and now there's laughter back in your home. Now that you can concentrate again, your grades have risen. God has healed your family from so many frightening things. You can only sit by the stream and murmur, "Thank you, God. Thank you. Thank you!" over and over.

Praise God at all times. We can praise him in the storm as his strength brings us through. Then we must praise him when the storm has passed and the sun shines again. "I love you, Lord, my strength. The Lord is my rock, my fortress and my deliverer; my God is my rock, in whom I take refuge, my shield and the horn of my salvation, my stronghold" (Psalm 18:1–2 TNIV). Take time—right now—to thank God for his many blessings.

Did You Know ...

there are at least 4,610 hymns that contain the word *praise*? Check out cyber-hymnal.org, which catalogs thousands of hymns. "He is your praise; he is your God, who performed for you those great and awesome wonders you saw with your own eyes" (Deuteronomy 10:21 TNIV).

More To Explore: Psalm 59:9-10

Girl Talk:

Can you list five things—both happy things and hard things—that you can thank God for right now? Then thank the Lord and praise his name!

God Talk:

 Lord, help me always remember to thank you for all you have done. Thank you for _____. I want to praise your name. You are an awesome God! Amen.

Mini-Quiz:

What famous king wrote so many songs praising God that Psalms is now the longest book in the Bible?

a. Solomon
b. King Tut
c. Jeroboam
d. David

Answer: d. David

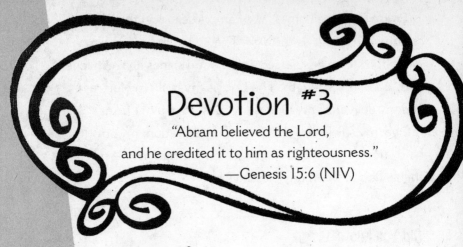

Devotion #3

"Abram believed the Lord,
and he credited it to him as righteousness."
—Genesis 15:6 (NIV)

Believing God

Because Abram believed the promises God gave to him, God said Abram was a righteous man. To be righteous means to honor God and live your life according to his will. When Abram believed God's promises, it honored God. God responded by declaring him righteous because of his belief.

Jamie had a hard time believing anyone. She'd heard her older brother declare he never took drugs—then watched him be arrested for drug abuse. Her dad had promised he'd be there forever—just a month before he walked out without an explanation. So when her mom promised one weekend that she'd take Saturday off and go with Jamie to an amusement park, Jamie muttered, "Yeah, I'll believe that when I see it." Her mom was hurt that Jamie didn't believe her. It didn't seem fair. She hadn't done anything to lose Jamie's confidence or make Jamie distrust her.

Even more so, God deserves our trust for being our all-loving Creator and giver of good gifts, and he wants us to believe him. "Without faith it is impossible to please God, because anyone who comes to him must believe that he exists and that he rewards those who earnestly seek him" (Hebrews 11:6 NIV). You don't just have faith (or trust) by itself. You have faith IN something or someone. The proper and most reliable place to put our faith is in God.

People will let you down. Sometimes it's on purpose, like when they make promises they don't intend to keep. Most often, people don't mean to disappoint you—they're just imperfect human beings. Put your trust in God instead of people. He will never let you down.

Did You Know ...

the hymn "Trust and Obey" was written following an evangelical crusade in 1887? John H. Sammis and Daniel B. Towner wrote the song. According to the refrain, we should "trust and obey, for there's no other way to be happy in Jesus, but to trust and obey."

More To Explore: Hebrews 11:1

Girl Talk:

Which people in your family do you trust? Do you find it hard to keep trusting? Do you have faith that God will never let you down?

God Talk:

Lord, sometimes it is hard for me to trust others. Help me to remember that you can always be trusted and that you will never let me down. Thank you.
Amen.

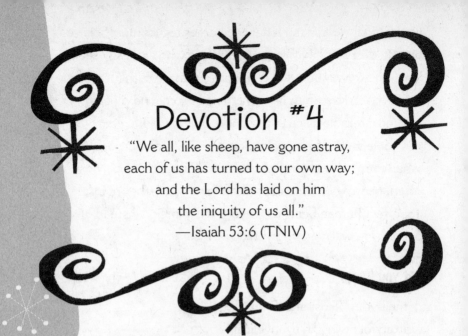

Devotion #4

"We all, like sheep, have gone astray,
each of us has turned to our own way;
and the Lord has laid on him
the iniquity of us all."
—Isaiah 53:6 (TNIV)

Baa, Baa, Black Sheep

Sheep aren't very smart. They wander off, get lost, and fall off cliffs. They require constant watching. Each of us has drifted away like a silly sheep. We have left God's well-marked paths to follow our own wrong ways. Even so, at the cross, God put all our guilt and sin on Jesus in order to bring us back into the fold.

Maybe you were raised in a Christian home, went to church faithfully, and were homeschooled until sixth grade. Then you go to public school. You expect the kids to make fun of you, but instead they invite you to games, parties, and movies. You know your parents wouldn't approve of the movies you're seeing, but you don't want to look judgmental. Anyway, the movies are pretty funny. Like a wandering sheep, you stray off a godly path. At one party, when someone produces some pills and other drugs, you nearly fall off the cliff. You come to your senses, though, and call your dad to pick you up. "I have wandered away like a lost sheep; come and find me, for I have not forgotten your commands" (Psalm 119:176 NLT). He's there in ten minutes. Sobbing in the car on the way home, you tell your dad what happened that night.

When you arrive home, your dad leans over and hugs you hard. "I'm so glad you called," he says. If *you've* wandered off the right path, it's never too late to go home. Even if you do not have an earthly father like this one, your heavenly Father always welcomes you back home.

Did You Know ...

if you're a follower of Jesus, "you were like sheep going astray, but now you have returned to the Shepherd and Overseer of your souls" (1 Peter 2:25 TNIV)?

More To Explore: Matthew 18:12–14

Girl Talk:

Have you ever wandered away from what you know is right? What happened? How can you get back on the path?

God Talk:

Lord, even though I know the right things to do, I don't always do them. I know you are always there welcoming me back. Please keep me near you. Amen.

Fun Factoid

A sheep's first instinct is to run, not fight. Maybe that explains why sheep have survived in the wild for hundreds of years.

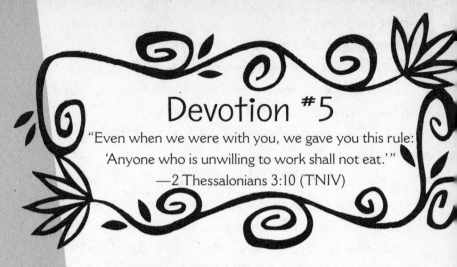

Devotion #5

"Even when we were with you, we gave you this rule: 'Anyone who is unwilling to work shall not eat.'"
—2 Thessalonians 3:10 (TNIV)

Don't Reward Wrong

In the apostle Paul's letter to the church, he reminded them how to treat those who wouldn't work. He said not to reward the lazy by feeding them food that others had worked to grow. It doesn't help to reward laziness. It only makes people lazier.

Lauren was sick of lazy classmates. She hated doing group projects where each person in the group got the same grade. She always ended up doing 80 percent of the work, no matter how many were in the group. Her current project on the Civil War was no different. The two boys in her group each promised to write a report and find some maps. By the day before the presentation, however, they'd done nothing. To keep from failing, Lauren stayed up most of that night, finding maps and information on the Internet, and then writing the boys' reports. She fumed the whole time—it was so unfair! The next day their group was called on first. Mrs. Sanders asked which student had done which part—and to show her their rough drafts and notes to prove it. The truth came out. Lauren got an A+, and the boys each got Fs. "I don't believe in rewarding poor behavior," Mrs. Sanders said.

Since ancient biblical times, there have been lazy people. "Sluggards do not plow in season; so at harvest time they look but find nothing" (Proverbs 20:4 TNIV). What responsible behavior should you adopt instead? "This should be your ambition: to live a quiet life, minding your own business and working with your hands, just as we commanded you before" (1 Thessalonians 4:11 NLT). Do work hard—and then enjoy the results of your labor.

Did You Know ...

the Bible says a lazy man might be getting too much rest and sleep? (See Proverbs 24:30–34.)

More To Explore: Proverbs 13:4

Girl Talk:

Think of the last project you worked on. How hard did you work? Are you proud of your efforts? If not, what can you do differently next time?

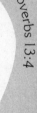

God Talk:

Lord, sometimes it's tempting to be lazy, but I know that's not what you want. Please help me work hard in everything I do. Amen.

Devotion #6

"Commit to the Lord whatever you do,
and he will establish your plans."
—Proverbs 16:3 (TNIV)

Success God's Way

Whatever job you need to do, give it to God. Trust that he will give you his ideas. He will help you set goals and succeed in the way he knows is best for you.

You're in sixth-grade band, and for your fund-raiser, you have to sell at least ten boxes of candy. There's only one problem: you hurry home every day to care for your mom, who's recovering from some surgery. You also watch your little sister and cook supper. There's no time to go door-to-door selling candy. Two days before the deadline, you've sold only one box—to your dad. "Lord, I trust you to show me what to do," you pray. You put your box of candy by the front door so you'll remember to take it back to school on Monday. But on Sunday, two ladies from church visit your mom, and when they leave, one lady asks about the candy. You explain about the fund-raiser, and the lady buys two boxes. That night, about an hour before bedtime, the doorbell rings again. Four people from church stand there. "We understand you're selling candy," one of the men says. "Do you have any left?" You nod, too surprised to speak. When they leave fifteen minutes later, your box is empty.

"Take delight in the Lord and he will give you the desires of your heart. Commit your way to the Lord; trust in him and he will do this" (Psalm 37:4–5 TNIV). God wants to plant his desires for you in your heart, so that he can fulfill them. He will make a way for you to succeed, even where there seems to be no way.

Did You Know ...

God made a way for Peter to keep preaching God's Word even after Herod put him in prison? An angel came to Peter, made his chains fall off, and they walked right out of prison! (Read Acts 12:5–7.) God can do anything!

More To Explore: Philippians 4:6

Girl Talk:

Have you ever been given a job that seemed impossible? How hard did you try to do the job? Did you ask God for help?

God Talk:

Lord, when things seem impossible, please remind me to call on you first. Only with your help can I do it. Thank you. Amen.

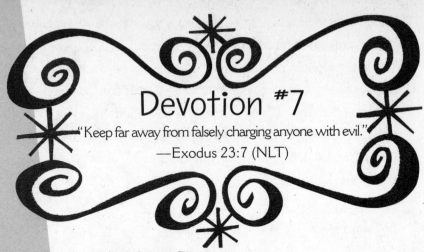

False Accusations

It's wrong to make false charges against anyone. Get your facts straight. Don't listen to others' accusations, and don't pass along rumors.

Elizabeth was walking by her neighbor's home when Mr. Jones ran out of the house. He raced to his car, squealed as he backed out of the driveway, and tore off down the street. Mrs. Jones came out on the front porch looking upset, but he was long gone. Elizabeth, embarrassed, hurried home. She told her sister that Mr. Jones was driving like a maniac, like someone who'd been drinking. She also reported that Mrs. Jones was really upset with him. Maybe they were getting a divorce.

That night at supper, Elizabeth repeated her story. Her mom scowled, then replied, "You've made some serious charges. And you couldn't be more wrong." Elizabeth's face grew warm as her mom explained what had happened. "Mrs. Jones called and asked us to pray for her husband's father. They got a call this afternoon that he'd had a heart attack. You witnessed Mr. Jones racing off to the hospital, hoping to see his father before he went into surgery." Ashamed of the rumor she'd started, Elizabeth hung her head.

People often jump to conclusions, many of them false. When you see something that makes you curious, don't try to be a mind reader. Don't assume bad motives or reasons for what people say or do. Then you'll be less likely to make false accusations. Wrong thinking and guesswork (like Elizabeth's) lead to making false charges. Instead, pray about things you see, and give people the benefit of the doubt. Then others will be more likely to do that for you!

Did You Know ...

the policy of tabloid publications is to spread anything they hear? Many of these "news" magazines at the checkout stands have been sued by celebrities who say the tabloids reported the story wrong or just made it up! Stay away from people who don't care about the truth. (See Proverbs 4:14–15.)

More To Explore: Exodus 23:1

Girl Talk:

Can you remember a time when you got carried away by what you saw or heard? Do you spread tales before you know the whole story?

God Talk:

Lord, sometimes it seems fun to have the scoop on someone, whether I know the whole story or not. Please help me keep my mouth quiet when I should. Amen.

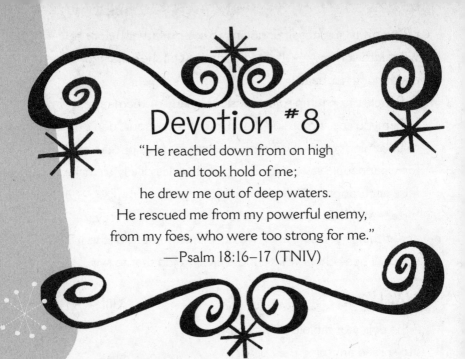

Devotion #8

"He reached down from on high
and took hold of me;
he drew me out of deep waters.
He rescued me from my powerful enemy,
from my foes, who were too strong for me."
—Psalm 18:16–17 (TNIV)

Call 9-1-1!

When David was being hunted down by his enemies, he cried out to God to save him. God reached down from heaven and rescued him. He pulled him out of deep trouble and snatched him away from the powerful enemies who hated him.

Maybe you aren't facing any enemies at school or in your neighborhood. Your enemy lives in your house. You were happy when your mom remarried, and you loved your stepdad. But with the remarriage came your older stepbrother, who seems to hate the new family. He takes his anger out on you. No matter how you try to avoid him when your parents are at work, he manages to kick or punch you several times a week. He threatens you with worse if you tell anyone.

But you know about God's rescuing David from his ene-mies. And you know that "God doesn't show partiality" (Acts 10:34 NLT). If God would rescue David, he would rescue you. You pray to be protected from your stepbrother and to have a safe home. You trust God to hear you and save you. One afternoon your stepdad arrives home unexpectedly from work and sees his son attack you. He steps in imme-diately. In the end, your stepbrother moves to his mom's house in another state, and peace settles over your home.

There are many millions of people on this earth. Why would God take time to rescue you? "He led me to a place of safety; he rescued me because he delights in me" (Psalm 18:19 NLT). He saves you because he loves you.

Did You Know ...

God rescued many others? He divided the Red Sea to save the Israelites. He used a prostitute and a rope to save two Israelite spies in Jericho.

More To Explore: Psalms 144:7; 40:1–3

Girl Talk:

Can you describe a time when you felt that you needed res-cuing? How did you solve the problem?

God Talk:

Lord, I feel scared when I think about _____. Please help calm my fears and rescue me from this situation. Thank you for always being there for me. Amen.

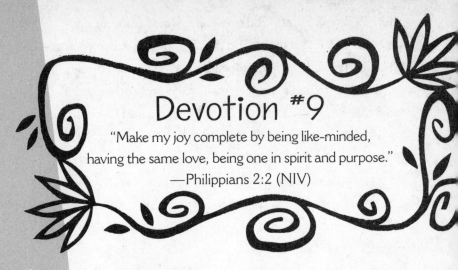

Devotion #9

"Make my joy complete by being like-minded,
having the same love, being one in spirit and purpose."
—Philippians 2:2 (NIV)

United as One

Believers have a common outlook on life based on knowing Jesus and living according to the Word of God. Followers of Christ should work together with one heart and one purpose.

Emily's family endured several shocks in the course of a month. Her dad's company went bankrupt, and he lost his job. When he couldn't find another one that paid as well, they sold their large home with a pool and moved into a tiny house. Then her mom discovered she was expecting another baby. Emily was in turmoil—until one evening they had a family roundtable discussion about their situation. "Loving God comes first," her dad said, "and then loving each other. If we pull together, we can make this work." The discussion that followed brought out different ideas for making money, cutting costs, and helping care for the baby when it arrived. There were many different ideas—but the family was like-minded about their purpose: loving God and loving one another.

Unity should exist among Christians. This doesn't mean thinking exactly alike on everything. It means having the common goal of working together and serving one another. "I appeal to you, brothers and sisters, in the name of our Lord Jesus Christ, that all of you agree with one another in what you say and that there be no divisions among you, but that you be perfectly united in mind and thought" (1 Corinthians 1:10 TNIV). Being unified comes with a great reward: God's presence in your life. "Be of good comfort, be of one mind, live in peace; and the God of love and peace will be with you" (2 Corinthians 13:11 NKJV). United we stand!

Did You Know ...

The Three Musketeers, by Alexandre Dumas, made popular a great line about unity? The Musketeer slogan was, "All for one, and one for all!"

Girl Talk:

Do you think your church family provides a united front? How can you improve on working together, both at church and at home?

More To Explore: Romans 12:16–18

God Talk:

Lord, I want to work better with my family. As much as depends on me, help me live with them in peace and find ways to love them and serve them. Amen.

"UNITY"
Harmony
In kinship
Christ at center
At peace
Love

Devotion #10

"When a bird sees a trap being set, it stays away."
—Proverbs 1:17 (NLT)

Trapped!

It's silly to set a trap right in front of a bird. It will fly away to avoid being caught. People need to learn a lesson from the birds! People often see danger, but ignore it.

You and Monica have been best friends for years, but something changes when you both start middle school. You sense that Monica isn't telling you the truth when she says she spends the whole evening at the library. When Monica claims that her new expensive bracelet is a gift from her grandmother, your stomach churns. Yet you ignore your suspicions and pretend to believe her. Later, when you're with Monica at the mall, the store detective grabs you both on the way out of the store. Terrified, you discover that Monica has shoplifted from the store, and because you're together, you're both in trouble.

Few things just "happen" to you. You nearly always receive advance warnings—comments from your friends or parents, gut instincts, and nudges from the Holy Spirit. Warnings alert you to danger. Maybe the first time you loaned your friend some money, she didn't pay it back. Or perhaps the first time you disagreed with a person, he screamed at you or called you names. Those are warning signs. If you keep going, you'll likely end up in trouble of some kind: losing more money or having a bully for a friend. Instead, "free yourself, like a gazelle from the hand of the hunter, like a bird from the snare of the fowler" (Proverbs 6:5 TNIV). Don't walk into a trap. Instead, get free!

Did You Know ...

using the color yellow to mean "take caution" comes from early seaports and ships? A yellow signal told the seamen to be careful when dropping anchor or that it was unsafe to leave port.

More To Explore: Jeremiah 5:26

Girl Talk:

Can you name some warning signs you've received lately? At school, at home, with friends? Pay attention to them, and pray for guidance.

God Talk:

Lord, I want to make the right choices. Please help me recognize any warning signs you send. Thank you for giving me those nagging feelings. Amen.

Fun Factoid

Using the color yellow to warn people to be cautious shows up everywhere: our streets, NASCAR, and the railroad. Even Japan uses yellow as a signal for caution in their street-marking system.

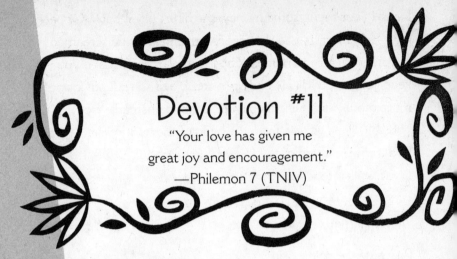

Devotion #11

*"Your love has given me
great joy and encouragement."*
—Philemon 7 (TNIV)

Way To Go!

When we love one another, we bring joy during
times of disappointment and hardship. Show your
love by giving a kind word and lifting someone else's
spirits.

Samantha wasn't athletic or pretty. She couldn't sing,
play an instrument, or create art. But Samantha was very
popular. Why? She loved others, and she showed it by
encouraging people. She cheered hard at the baseball games.
She attended her classmates' concerts and complimented
them on their band and vocal solos. She noticed when people
looked sad and did her best to cheer them up. She didn't do
it to be popular, but people loved having her around.

How can you be an encourager? Notice when
someone tries hard to accomplish something.
Say, "Great job!" or "Way to go!" Also, find
someone going through a hard experience
that you have been through yourself. If
your parents were divorced a few years
ago, and a classmate is now coping with
it, you can offer encouragement. Let her
know that things will get better. You could

also tell her about the comfort you received from God, who is the best encourager of all: "the Father of compassion and the God of all comfort, who comforts us in all our troubles, so that we can comfort those in any trouble with the comfort we ourselves receive from God" (2 Corinthians 1:3–4 TNIV). Make it your goal to encourage someone in your family or at school every day. One surprising benefit will be that your own joy will greatly increase.

Did You Know ...

the word *encourage* implies acts of strengthening another person? Who can you strengthen and comfort today with an encouraging word?

More To Explore: 2 Corinthians 7:13

Girl Talk:

How often do you notice the hard work of others? Do you go the extra mile and encourage them? If so, how? Or do you feel too self-conscious?

God Talk:

Lord, thank you for the gift of encouragement. I want to use it more to lift up others. Please help me find ways to encourage those around me. Amen.

More Ways To Encourage:

- When you offer help, be specific. "Would it help you if I _____?"
- Write someone a note, and tell her you're praying for her.
- Give someone a hug, a high-five, or a pat on the back (if it's okay with them).

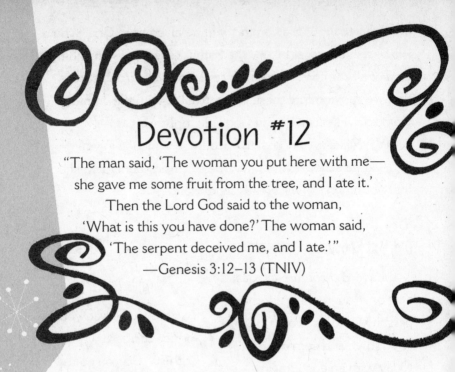

Devotion #12

"The man said, 'The woman you put here with me—
she gave me some fruit from the tree, and I ate it.'
Then the Lord God said to the woman,
'What is this you have done?' The woman said,
'The serpent deceived me, and I ate.'"
—Genesis 3:12–13 (TNIV)

Who? Me?

In the garden of Eden, Adam and Eve could eat the fruit from any tree they liked—except one. But Eve disobeyed God's command and ate the forbidden fruit. Adam also ate it. When God confronted them, Adam blamed both God and the woman for his own sin. ("It was *the woman* that *you* gave me who brought me the fruit.") Eve had her own excuse, and she blamed the serpent. ("*He* tricked me.")

You might find yourself making excuses for your problems too. Maybe you're naturally shy, and your goal is to blend in and not be noticed. However, you're very lonely this way. "Everyone's so unfriendly," you tell your mom. "They stare right past me!" Only after an honest discussion about your behavior at school can you see your part in the problem. You admit that you don't look at or talk to people. You avoid groups and disappear to be by yourself. Finally you decide to take responsibility and change. After a few weeks of forcing yourself to talk to your classmates, things change. Your unfriendly classmates magically transform into fun friends!

The game of "poor me" and "it's your fault" got started in the garden of Eden. To this day, people blame their problems on others. They blame their parents, their teachers, and the world in order to shift the responsibility. Some people prefer to believe that something else is controlling the outcome of their lives. However, we must stop blaming others and study our own behavior instead. Take personal responsibility for change. Then you can turn around and head in the direction of God's good plan for your life.

Did You Know ...

the Israelites blamed God many times for their troubles, even after they were delivered from Egypt? Read Exodus 16:1–5.

More To Explore: Genesis 3:6

Girl Talk:

Think about a recent problem you had. Where did you place the blame? Did you put the responsibility in the right place?

God Talk:

Lord, it's so easy to blame others when things go wrong. Help me to take responsibility when it's my fault. Thank you for loving me no matter what I do. Amen.

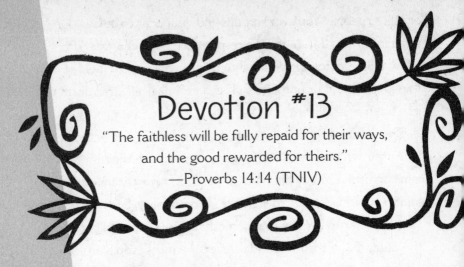

Devotion #13

"The faithless will be fully repaid for their ways,
and the good rewarded for theirs."
—Proverbs 14:14 (TNIV)

Going Backward?

People who follow God for a while but later return
to their old ways of sinful living are sometimes
referred to as "backsliders." A backslider's life is eventually filled with negative consequences. People who
stay faithful to God also receive their reward—a life filled
with joy in their work and peace in their relationships.

Megan was sad when her friend Tia stopped coming to
youth group, where they had both sung with the praise band.
Megan continued to sing on youth night, and eventually the
band was asked to perform in church. Months later, the
group made a music CD. Bit by bit, Megan's dream of
being a Christian vocal artist was coming true. And
Tia? The crowd she hung out with preferred parties to church, and one night Tia was injured
in a car accident. The driver was underage
and drunk. Tia would be in therapy for
months to regain the use of her legs.

What happened to Tia was largely
the result of her own actions. Actions
have consequences, either positive or

negative. If a farmer planted weed seeds in his field, he would harvest a worthless crop of weeds. It wouldn't be God doing anything to him. It would be the result of his own actions. "Your wickedness will punish you; your backsliding will rebuke you" (Jeremiah 2:19 TNIV). Sinful living has its own consequences—although God will use those consequences as ways to help us mature.

So pull out the weeds in your life. Plant healthy seeds in their place. Then get ready for a harvest of blessings!

Did You Know ...

the concept of seeds is used throughout the Bible? Even with faith only the size of a mustard seed, we can do great things. (See Matthew 17:20.) The Word of God is referred to as seed in Mark 4.

More To Explore: Mark 4:3–20

Girl Talk:

What weeds are choking out good decisions in your life? Ask God to help you get rid of those weeds.

God Talk:

Lord, there are some things in my life that are choking my walk with you. Please help me get rid of them and plant healthy, godly activities in their place. Amen.

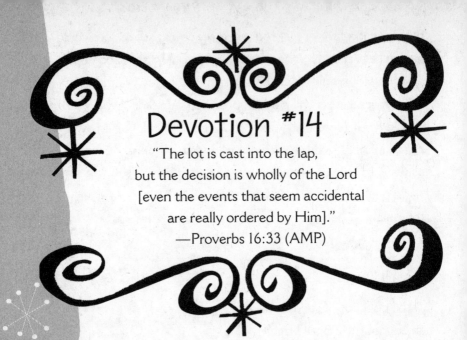

Devotion #14

"The lot is cast into the lap,
but the decision is wholly of the Lord
[even the events that seem accidental
are really ordered by Him]."
—Proverbs 16:33 (AMP)

Roll The Dice!

In biblical times, the lot may have been several pebbles
held in the fold of a robe and then drawn out or shaken to
the ground. It was a common practice for making decisions,
like throwing dice today or flipping a coin. However, God—
not chance or luck—is in control of how things turn out.

You love the new house you're moving into. Finally you'll
get a bedroom of your own, apart from Emily, your younger
sister. One bedroom has a tiny window, but the corner
bedroom has two huge windows with trees right outside. In your mind, you've already decorated that
room. When your family moves in, though,
Emily wants that bedroom and refuses to
take the other room. Your parents say
that since you're the oldest, you can
have first choice. "That's not fair!"
Emily cries. You think about it for a
moment. "Let's try something that is fair,"

you say. "Dad, flip a coin for us, okay? Emily, do you want heads or tails?" You trust that God is in control. If he wants you to have the corner room, you'll get it.

This is what people in biblical times did when they cast lots. What was the point of casting lots to make decisions? It was fair—and it stopped people from fighting. "Casting lots causes contentions to cease, and keeps the mighty apart" (Proverbs 18:18 NKJV). The next time you and another person want the same thing—the last piece of pizza, choosing the TV channel, or picking a movie—try "casting lots" and bring peace to the situation.

Did You Know ...

by casting lots, Jonah was discovered to be the cause of the great storm? In this case, all the people on board drew straws to see which of them had offended the gods. Jonah drew the short straw. (See Jonah 1:7.)

Girl Talk:

What is something you and your siblings or friends tend to pick fights about? Would casting lots be a fair way to end the disagreement?

More To Explore: Nehemiah 11:1

God Talk:

Lord, thank you for a simple and fair way to make minor decisions that could cause fights. Help me remember that I do not have to always have my own way. Amen.

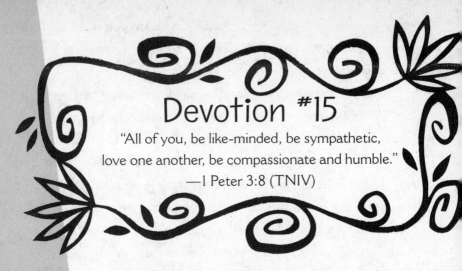

Devotion #15

"All of you, be like-minded, be sympathetic,
love one another, be compassionate and humble."
—1 Peter 3:8 (TNIV)

Caring for One Another

Believers should strive to live in harmony with others. Be sensitive toward each other's feelings, loving one another with tender hearts and humble minds.

Sarah had a kind and generous heart by nature, and she didn't understand why other kids had trouble getting along—until Tiffany moved to town. Tiffany was in Sarah's grade at school, and she attended youth group and Bible study every week. But she didn't just participate like everyone else. She blew into the room, like a gust of wind that unsettled everything. She was loud, thought she knew it all, and was determined to change everything so it was done "right." Bossy and opinionated—that described Tiffany perfectly, Sarah thought. Living in harmony and being sympathetic to such an inflated ego strained Sarah's patience. Sarah would have preferred avoiding Tiffany altogether, but she knew Jesus wanted her to be kind and loving toward Tiffany. *Help me, Lord*, Sarah prayed as she acted in kind ways. Over several months, Sarah's heart slowly lined up with her loving actions. In the end, Tiffany became Sarah's close friend.

We are to be sympathetic to others. "When others are happy, be happy with them. If they are sad, share their sorrow. Live in harmony with each other" (Romans 12:15–16 NLT). Being kind and loving toward one another isn't just a good idea. It's a commandment from God, and it applies whether we feel like being compassionate or not. Show love and kindness to others—it will come back to you multiplied many times over!

Did You Know ...

the Bible says we'll know we have passed from death to life if we have love for each other? (See 1 John 3:14.)

More To Explore: Luke 10:30–35

Girl Talk:

Are there any people in your life you have a hard time getting along with? Why do you think they are the way they are? Think of one way to care for them today.

God Talk:

Lord, I know you want me to do my part to live in peace with everyone. Sometimes I have a hard time with _____. Please help me be more kind and loving toward this person. Thank you. Amen.

Mini-Quiz:

What doesn't belong with harmony?
a. kindness
b. sharing
c. backstabbing
d. encouragement

Answer: c. backstabbing

Devotion #16

"Let our lives lovingly express truth [in all things,
speaking truly, dealing truly, living truly].
Enfolded in love, let us grow up in
every way and in all things."
—Ephesians 4:15 (AMP)

Nothing but the Truth

Believers should have a truthful and loving way of dealing with others. Don't express the truth in a harsh way. Day by day, and year by year, let Jesus make you more and more like him. Believers who do this show that they are growing up (or maturing) in their faith.

Maybe you have two friends. They both tell you the truth, but one feels warm and caring, while the other girl's "truth" cuts deep. When you all try out for the track team, Girlfriend #1 says to you, "You're a natural for long-distance running. You hardly broke a sweat running the mile!" Fake Friend #2 also speaks the truth: "You know, your short legs are stubby, so don't even think about hurdles. You'll fall flat on your face." Both girls spoke the truth, but only one spoke the truth in love.

What are some signs of growth in believers? They speak words of truth, but in a loving manner. They aren't brutal, then claim, "I'm just telling the truth. Don't be so touchy." Their love is also honest. "Love must be sincere" (Romans 12:9 TNIV). No faking allowed! True Christian love is open and genuine, not two-faced and phony. A growing Christian backs up her loving words with action. "Let us not love in word or in tongue, but in deed and in truth" (1 John 3:18 NKJV). As you grow, let love guide you—in your thoughts, words, and actions. "God is love. Whoever lives in love lives in God, and God in them" (1 John 4:16 TNIV). Be enfolded in God's love today!

Did You Know ...

Ruth was a mature believer of God who kept her word, was always gentle and loving, and showed her love in her actions? God blessed her by making her the great-grandmother of David. (See Matthew 1:5–6.)

More To Explore: Psalm 32:2

Girl Talk:

How do you speak the truth? Are you loving or brutal? The next time you speak the truth, let it be gentle, and follow it up with action.

God Talk:

Lord, I want to grow in my relationship with you. Please help me be always truthful, but also always kind and gentle. Thank you. Amen.

Devotion #17

"By standing firm you will gain life."
—Luke 21:19 (NIV)

Solid as Rock

Jesus told his disciples that their lives would be rough sometimes. During tests and trials, we should stand firm. Only by patiently enduring will we have eternal life. So stand firm to the end—such perseverance is a sure sign of your salvation.

Michelle's sixth-grade year was one long trial after another. In church camp the summer before, she was challenged to be bolder in her faith. So she decided to "come out of hiding." Until now, she never mentioned church at school. She didn't explain why she skipped certain movies or didn't dress in the popular tight tees and miniskirts. Michelle just tried to be nice and blend in. She never had to defend her faith—because no one knew she had any. Then in sixth grade, she wore her cross necklace and "What Would Jesus Do?" T-shirt. She got noticed— and teased. When Michelle took stands on issues, she was often alone. But this was her attitude throughout: "I remain confident of this: I will see the goodness of the Lord in the land of the living. Wait for the Lord; be strong and take heart and wait for the Lord" (Psalm 27:13–14 TNIV). She put her trust in God and focused on him instead of those who ridiculed her. "Be still before the Lord and wait patiently for him; do not fret when people succeed in their ways, when they carry out their wicked schemes" (Psalm 37:7 TNIV).

Eventually, two girls told Michelle they were Christians too, and Michelle made two excellent friends. "And so after waiting patiently, Abraham received what was promised" (Hebrews 6:15 TNIV). Standing firm through tests and trials will also see the promises of God become reality in your own life.

Did You Know ...

the Corn Flakes had trouble being patient with Phoebe in *Sophie Tracks a Thief*? Dr. Peter told them, "Just because it doesn't look like it's working doesn't mean it isn't." We need to be patient while waiting for people to change.

Girl Talk:

Have you had any trying times lately? What do you think God might be trying to teach you?

More To Explore: Psalm 40:1

God Talk:

Lord, doing the right thing is not always popular. Please help me to be patient and stay focused on you. I know that with you beside me, I can't go wrong. Amen.

Devotion #18

"If you keep my commands,
you will remain in my love,
just as I have kept my Father's commands
and remain in his love."
—John 15:10 (TNIV)

If

We are to follow Jesus' example. Just as he was obedient to his Father, we are to obey Jesus. Obedience and love go hand in hand. And what a promise is attached to this obedience! We will live in Jesus' love in the same way that he rests in God's love.

You've been a believer since you were ten years old. You truly love Jesus more each year, and you talk to him often. Jesus is your constant companion and best friend as you move with your military dad from place to place. You love the Lord, but there are times you just don't want to do what Jesus says. You don't always want to obey your dad, especially when he barks at you as if you're one of his soldiers. You don't always want to give part of your allowance in the offering plate; sometimes you want to buy something for yourself with all the money. But you know that if you really love Jesus like you claim, you'll obey what he tells you to do.

Jesus made it very plain. "If you love me, keep my commands" (John 14:15 TNIV). Obedience and love go together, whether we like it or not. Don't tell Jesus (or others) that you love the Lord if you're not willing to do what he tells you to do. "Whoever has my commands and keeps them is the one who loves me. Anyone who loves me will be loved by my Father, and I too will love them and show myself to them" (John 14:21 TNIV). When you obey the Lord, he pours out such love on you. As you grow in this love, something wonderful happens. Obedience becomes a habit—and a joy!

Did You Know ...

eleven different places in the Bible mention both loving and obeying God in the same verse? (See, for example, John 14:15, 21; 15:10; and 1 John 2:5.)

More To Explore: 1 John 2:5–6

Girl Talk:

How often do you say that you love God, even though you're not doing what he asks? What is one thing that you know he wants you to do, but you're having trouble obeying?

God Talk:

Lord, I want to better prove my love for you by obeying your desires for me. Please help me follow you every day. Amen.

Devotion #19

"Lot chose that land for himself . . . After Lot was gone, the Lord said to Abram, 'Look as far as you can see in every direction. I am going to give all this land to you and your offspring as a permanent possession.'"
—Genesis 13:11, 14–15 (NLT)

Letting The Lord Choose

After Lot chose the best-looking land for himself, he and his uncle Abram parted ways. When Lot was gone, God told Abram to look in all directions as far as he could. God gave Abram's descendants (family) all the land that Abram could see! Lot chose for himself, and it was the beginning of his downfall. (It caused Lot to live on the well-watered plains of Jordan near the wicked city of Sodom.) Abram allowed God to choose for him, and later his descendants ended up in possession of the Promised Land.

The first week in her new middle school, Melissa watched kids quietly. She finally decided which group she wanted to belong to, and she planned how to get them to accept her. They finally did, but this group's activities landed Melissa in trouble. One weekend everything blew up in her face. Finally Melissa prayed, "Lord, I guess I don't know how to choose good friends. You can see into their hearts. Please bring me the friends you want me to have." Melissa was lonely for a few weeks, but then she was paired in a flute duet with a girl she truly liked. Later she shared an assigned spot in the science lab with another girl who turned out to be a believer.

When you let God choose for you—whether it's friends, clothes, or extracurricular activities—you'll end up with God's best. Be patient. Continue to pray while you wait. Don't get in a hurry and settle for less than the Promised Land God has in mind for you.

Did You Know ...

our country can be changed by the choices we make? In America, the decisions are made by the people (or the people they elect).

God Talk:

Lord, I love getting to have a choice, but I don't always choose what's best for me. Please help me to always pray before choosing anything.

Amen.

More To Explore: Genesis 19:15–17

Girl Talk:

How often do you talk with God before making decisions? Is it hard to be patient and wait to see what God wants you to do? How can you make the waiting easier?

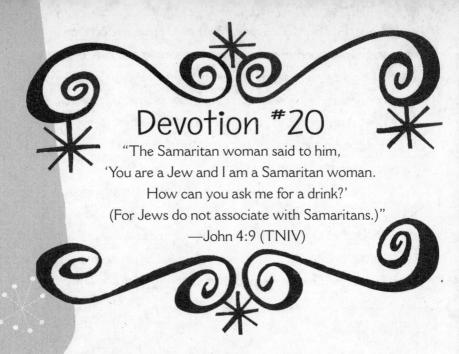

Devotion #20

"The Samaritan woman said to him,
'You are a Jew and I am a Samaritan woman.
How can you ask me for a drink?'
(For Jews do not associate with Samaritans.)"
—John 4:9 (TNIV)

Are You Talking To Me?

The Samaritan woman drawing water at the well was surprised when Jesus asked her for a drink. At that time, Jews refused to associate with Samaritans. (Jews believed they would become "unclean" if they used a drinking vessel handled by a Samaritan.) Also, women were usually ignored. "Just then his disciples returned and were surprised to find him talking with a woman" (John 4:27 TNIV). Jesus broke tradition by talking to a Samaritan and a woman. He didn't consider her "beneath" him.

You learn about prejudice when your family moves. You never felt out of place while living in Texas, but when your family relocates to a small town in Minnesota, you're the only Hispanic student in your school. Most kids ignore you. Some treat you like you have a contagious disease. A few call you names. Being the target of discrimination and bigotry is more hurtful than you ever would have guessed. Two years later, your family moves back to Texas. You absolutely love being "home," but you've changed. From now on, you're careful to never make another prejudiced comment. You've learned firsthand the pain it can cause.

Certain people believe they are worth more than others. God's Word, however, has strong words for such people: "Do not think of yourself more highly than you ought, but rather think of yourself with sober judgment, in accordance with the faith God has distributed to each of you" (Romans 12:3 TNIV). God's Word clearly says that your worth isn't in your nationality or the color of your skin. Instead, judge yourself by the strength of your faith in God. That's what really matters.

Did You Know ...

the Jews were mocked when trying to rebuild the wall around Jerusalem? (See Nehemiah 4:1–2.)

More To Explore: Acts 10:28

Girl Talk:

Have you ever treated someone differently because of how they looked? Are you sometimes treated differently because of the way you look? How does that feel?

God Talk:

Lord, I don't want to treat others differently or badly. It's hard not to follow the crowd, but I know I can follow you instead—with your help. Thank you. Amen.

Devotion #21

"Be on your guard; stand firm in the faith;
be courageous; be strong. Do everything in love."
—1 Corinthians 16:13–14 (TNIV)

On Guard!

Life can throw some frightening things at you—
totally out of the blue. Be ready, and stand true to
what you believe. Be strong and brave in the faith
God has given you. Everything you do must be done
with love.

Rosa knew about frightening things. Her mom remarried
three years after Rosa's dad left them. Rosa grew to love her
stepdad and stepsister. Just when they seemed like a real family, crisis struck again. Rosa's mom was diagnosed with a disease that would eventually confine her to a wheelchair.

Rosa's own faith wavered, but in the coming weeks she
learned about courage and trust from watching her
parents. They stood true to what they believed:
that God was good ALL the time; that he'd
allowed this for a purpose, that he had
everything under control, and that they
could trust him. No matter what.

God wouldn't command you to do
something unless he was willing to help
you do it. During a crisis or difficult time,

simply "standing firm" doesn't sound like much to accomplish, but it is. Satan will try to knock you down, but keep on standing. Say over and over—out loud—"God loves me, and I can trust him." Do it as long as it takes to build your faith up. God will move when he knows the time is right, when he's accomplished his purpose in the situation. "Wait for the Lord; be strong and take heart and wait for the Lord" (Psalm 27:14 TNIV). When life is hard, lean even harder on the Lord. He'll never let you down.

Did You Know ...

you can't be strong by yourself, but your strength has to come from the Lord? (See Ephesians 6:10.)

More To Explore: Colossians 4:2

Girl Talk:

Did you ever think standing still and strong could be so tiring and disheartening? Who can you ask for support as you stand strong?

God Talk:

Lord, I want to be strong for you. Please give me the strength to do what is right and not budge. Amen.

Fun Factoid

Lance Armstrong has a great slogan, "Live Strong," that goes with his efforts to fund cancer research. Maybe your new slogan could be "Stay Strong!"

Devotion #22

"Get rid of all bitterness, rage and anger, brawling and slander, along with every form of malice."
—Ephesians 4:31 (TNIV)

Anger Management?

There is no place for bitterness and anger in your life. Followers of Jesus should not speak harsh words to people or attack another person's character. Avoid noisy disagreements and fighting. Don't even wish evil on others. Such things have no place in the life of a believer.

Maybe you know all about fighting and rage. You're angry about things happening at home: a divorce, needing to move, having much less money. You hold in the anger at home, but it "leaks" out at school. At first it's in little ways with your friends. But when it increases and you snap at your teachers, you land in detention. In the end, the principal and the guidance counselor decide you should attend "anger management" classes. The classes will teach you how to control your anger, how to keep it from making you blow up at people. At the class, you're taught to explode in safe places, such as by hitting a pillow and screaming alone in your bedroom. The instructor wants you to transfer your anger energy into some other object.

Is that how the Bible says to deal with our anger? No. It doesn't say manage it. The Bible is very clear. It says get rid of it. "Now you must also rid yourselves of all such things as these: anger, rage, malice, slander, and filthy language from your lips" (Colossians 3:8 TNIV). Noisy disagreements and fighting only lead to further trouble. Avoid them too. "Don't have anything to do with foolish and stupid arguments, because you know they produce quarrels" (2 Timothy 2:23 TNIV). You can't do this alone. Give your anger to God. Ask him for help (many times a day, if necessary) until the anger is gone.

Did You Know ...

the Bible tells us to get rid of our anger before the end of the day? Ephesians 4:26 says, "Do not let the sun go down while you are still angry" (NIV).

Girl Talk:

What do you do when you get angry? Bottle it up? Let it loose on others? Something else? Do you ever ask God to take the anger away? Try it!

More To Explore: Matthew 18:21-22

God Talk:

Lord, sometimes it's hard to control my anger. Help me get rid of it. I don't want it poisoning my life anymore. Thank you. Amen.

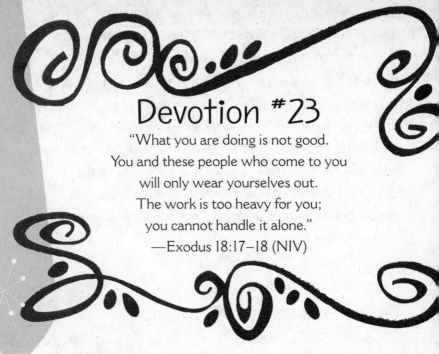

Devotion #23

"What you are doing is not good.
You and these people who come to you
will only wear yourselves out.
The work is too heavy for you;
you cannot handle it alone."
—Exodus 18:17–18 (NIV)

HeLp! HeLp!

Moses tried to handle all the questions and problems of several million Israelite people. From morning to night, he wore himself out listening to all their problems himself. It was too much. He couldn't handle it alone. He needed a plan to share the work with others.

Amanda also took on too much work. When her science class had team projects, she wanted to do an excellent job—and the others let her. She organized the meetings, did the research, typed the reports, and made the displays. When her youth group collected food for the homeless, Amanda went door-to-door every night after school and all day Saturday. She carted the canned goods to the church in her brother's wagon. She went along to deliver food to the shelter downtown. The following week, due to exhaustion and a weakened immune system, she caught a nasty virus. Like Moses, Amanda meant well, but taking on too much responsibility hurt her.

We need to use wisdom when agreeing to jobs. If you "bite off more than you can chew," you may end up sick (and unable to do all you promised). If your job turns out to be more time-consuming than you expected, it's all right to ask for help. Amanda needed to learn that she couldn't do it all. Sometimes we feel if we don't do it all, it won't get done right. Sometimes that's true—but usually it's not. We can let others help. It's great to work hard, but find a healthy balance.

Did You Know ...

overworking to be perfect has many negative side effects besides getting sick? It can lead to low self-esteem, guilt, and even depression.

More To Explore: Acts 6:1–4

Girl Talk:

Do you like to take charge of projects? Do you feel pressure to do everything right all by yourself? How can God help you?

God Talk:

Lord, sometimes I worry too much about how perfect something should be. Please help me remember to ask for help and for your guidance. Amen.

Beauty 101:

Worrying too much about getting something just right? You could be setting yourself up for early frown lines on your forehead. Relax your face and pray instead of worrying.

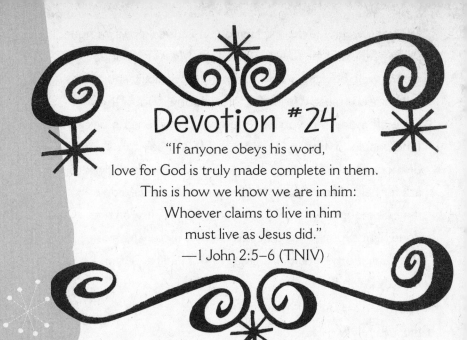

Devotion #24

"If anyone obeys his word,
love for God is truly made complete in them.
This is how we know we are in him:
Whoever claims to live in him
must live as Jesus did."
—1 John 2:5–6 (TNIV)

FALSE CLAIMS

Many inside and outside the church claim to love God. But do they pass the test? Those who obey God's Word are the ones who really do love him. That is the way to know whether or not we are his followers. Those who claim to be followers should live their lives as Christ did.

You remember the summer you accepted Jesus as your savior in vacation Bible school, along with your two best friends. You attended Sunday school together for years. But now that you're in middle school, you find excuses not to go. You stop giving offerings or reading your Bible. You want to see movies that your new friends see, so you begin sneaking out and lying about where you go. Your parents don't trust the kids you now want to hang out with, so you lie about that too. If anyone pins you down about your relationship with Jesus, you always say, "Oh, yeah, I'm a Christian." But you know your behavior says otherwise. You stopped obeying God's Word, and it doesn't bother you—unless you get caught. "No one who lives in him keeps on sinning. No one who continues to sin has either seen him or known him" (1 John 3:6 TNIV).

Be sure that if you say you're a follower of Jesus that you actually have the desire to follow him and grow in your relationship with him. And choose your friends accordingly. You can't—and shouldn't—judge whether someone is saved or not, but a person's lifestyle can be one good indication. Choose friends whose actions match what they say they believe.

Did You Know ...

Saul, the first king of Israel, did not follow the Lord's instructions? Saul did what he thought was best, not what God said to do. God was sorry that he had installed Saul as king. (See 1 Samuel 15:11.)

More To Explore: John 15:4–5

Girl Talk:

Think of your actions the last few weeks. Would God say that you obey him? Why or why not?

God Talk:

Lord, my actions don't always match what I say I believe. I want to follow you every day, not rely on myself or others. Please help me do that. Amen.

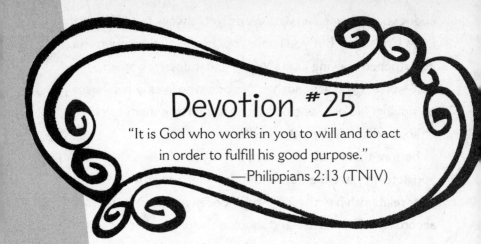

Devotion #25

"It is God who works in you to will and to act
in order to fulfill his good purpose."
—Philippians 2:13 (TNIV)

The Power Source

Believers must depend on God for their strength.
You can't live a godly life on your own. For God is
working in you, giving you the desire to obey him.
Then he gives you the energy and the power to do what
pleases him.

Alexis had great intentions for her summer job babysitting
three small neighborhood children. Their mom didn't want
them watching much TV, but instead to play at the park, go
swimming, and go to the library for story time. When Alexis
accepted the job, it sounded like fun! Imagine getting paid to
go to the pool! It was a shock to discover how much hard
work was involved in "playing" with kids. At the pool
Alexis didn't lay out with her friends—she enter-
tained for endless hours in the baby pool. At
the library, Alexis didn't browse through
the stacks of novels—she tried to keep
the baby from eating the board books
and screaming. At the park, she never
sat down—she pushed two kids on the
swings while keeping the baby from eating

sand. "I quit," Alexis finally told their mom. "I haven't got the strength."

Instead of leaning on her own strength, Alexis needed to ask God to work through her. Once she prayed, God gave Alexis the desire to do an excellent job of babysitting, along with the energy to do the work. Believe God for the power to do the job—and do it well.

Did You Know ...

you never have to rely on your own strength to do a job God has asked you to do? "I can do all things through Christ who strengthens me" (Philippians 4:13 NKJV).

God Talk:

Lord, I want to do great things for you. Please give me the motivation and energy to do everything you want me to do. Amen.

Girl Talk:

Are you trying to do a job that has exhausted you? Are you trying to do the job in your own strength? Or, perhaps, is it a job that God never asked you to do in the first place? If you're doing what God wants, ask him for help. He'll give it!

More To Explore: Hebrews 13:20-21

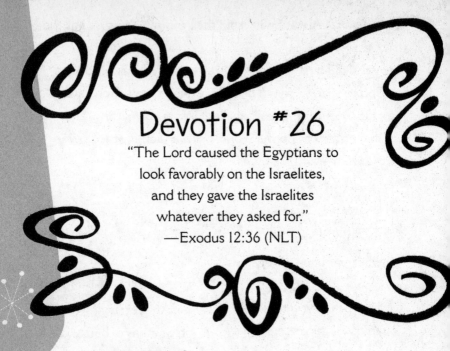

Devotion #26

"The Lord caused the Egyptians to
look favorably on the Israelites,
and they gave the Israelites
whatever they asked for."
—Exodus 12:36 (NLT)

God Bless You!

When it was time for the Israelites to leave their slavery behind in Egypt, God did a marvelous thing for them. He caused their former owners, the Egyptians, to like the slaves so much that they gave the slaves whatever they wanted to take with them! God can make even your enemies so pleased with you that they want to help you.

You wish *your* enemy would do that! You're sick of being picked on at school. You have no idea why Jason, the class clown, has singled you out, but he's made fun of you all year. You tried ignoring him, as your teacher suggested. You stood up to him and demanded that he stop it, as your dad suggested. You're tempted to call him names back, as your best friend suggests. Finally, you give up and do what you should have done in the first place:

you pray. You ask God to change Jason's heart and cause him to be friendly to you. Every time he picks on you, you pray again. Slowly, over a matter of weeks, Jason stops making fun of you. One day when you drop your books, you're astounded when Jason stops and picks them up for you.

God can change the hearts of people. When you work hard to gain approval from people yourself, you often have to keep working constantly in order to keep their approval. On the other hand, when God gives you favor with people, you can simply enjoy it. Live the kind of obedient life God requires. Then pray for favor with people. Relax and let God make it happen in his time.

Did You Know ...

even when Joseph was sold into slavery in Egypt, God caused the king of Egypt to be kind and generous with Joseph? (See Acts 7:9–10.)

More To Explore: Daniel 1:9

Girl Talk:

Is there someone in your life you just can't seem to please? What things have you tried? Have you asked God for help?

God Talk:

Lord, I don't know what to do about _____. Please give me favor with this person. Please show me the way to respond. Thank you. Amen.

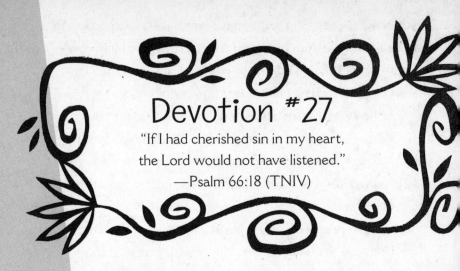

Devotion #27

"If I had cherished sin in my heart,
the Lord would not have listened."
—Psalm 66:18 (TNIV)

First Do This...

David (who wrote many of the psalms) knew that
if he had treasured sin in his life—held on to it—
the Lord would not have heard his prayers. Cherished
sin needs to become confessed sin if you want God to
listen to you.

Nicole's older sister Steph caused constant turmoil in the
family. At sixteen, Steph demanded to run her own life. She
rebelled against everything: going to church, her curfew, doing
homework, and any rule their parents set. In high school, she'd
made new friends, and these friends liked to party. Nicole
shared a room with her sister, who often dragged in reeking
of alcohol and cigarettes. When Steph's boyfriend
dumped her, Steph was stunned and hurt. Nicole
heard Steph pray for God to bring him back.
When it didn't happen, she blamed God
and continued to rebel. Nicole shook her
head. How could Steph expect God to
hear her prayer—even if he wanted to
help her—when she continued in her sinful and rebellious lifestyle?

Nicole's sister is no different from many people. They have accepted Christ's death on the cross and forgiveness for their sins, but they rebel against the Lord's instructions for daily living. Then, when an emergency strikes, they quickly call on the Lord and expect instant answers to their prayers. God will certainly help any believer caught in the grip of sin who truly wants to be set free. But if you're cherishing certain sins in your life—and intend to continue in that lifestyle—then confess it right now. Seek forgiveness and change. Then you'll be in a position for God to hear your prayers.

Did You Know ...

wanting to rebel starts as early as at one year of age? When a child is learning that she is independent of her parents, one of her first words is "no."

More To Explore: Psalm 51:10-12

Girl Talk:

Is there any sinful habit in your life that's hard to give up? How do you think it might be keeping you from growing with God?

God Talk:

Lord, I struggle with _____. It's hard to give it up, but I want to please you. Help me throw this sin away and get closer to you. Amen.

Devotion #28

"Now to him who is able to do immeasurably
more than all we ask or imagine,
according to his power that is at work within us . . ."
—Ephesians 3:20 (TNIV)

Beyond Our Dreams

If you are a believer, God's mighty power is working in you. By his power, he is able to accomplish more than we would ever dare to ask or hope. He can carry out his plans for our lives and achieve things beyond our biggest desires, thoughts, or dreams.

Maybe you're having terrible trouble understanding your subjects in school. You read the same paragraphs over and over, but can't understand the meaning. Your grades go from As to Ds. Whereas you once enjoyed school, you now dread it. "Dear Lord, please help me," you pray every night. "I don't want to flunk fifth grade." One day, a young woman visits your school and gives you some tests. She discovers that an accident the year before, when you hit her head, has left you with a learning disability. The young woman offers to teach you some special ways to read and learn. "Then I won't flunk?" you ask hopefully. The young woman smiles and says, "It will be even better than that." Within six months, your grades are as high as before the accident.

Sometimes when we pray for God's help, we hope for just enough help to get by. Yet "no eye has seen, no ear has heard, and no mind has imagined what God has prepared for those who love him" (1 Corinthians 2:9 NLT). God doesn't just want us to have a life in which we barely survive. He wants us to grow stronger and thrive. So pray—and expect answers beyond your wildest dreams!

Did You Know ...

Esther, a beautiful Jewish orphan, was given more by God than she could ever have dreamed? God put her in a position of power as queen of Media-Persia. She saved her people by alerting the king to a death plot. (See Esther 8:3.)

Girl Talk:

How do you pray? Do you pray for just a little help, hoping that God will answer? Or do you pray for the best that God can give you? What determines how you pray?

More To Explore: 1 Timothy 1:14

God Talk:

Lord, I know you have almighty power, but sometimes I am afraid to ask for it. Please be with me and help me live life to the fullest. Thank you! Amen.

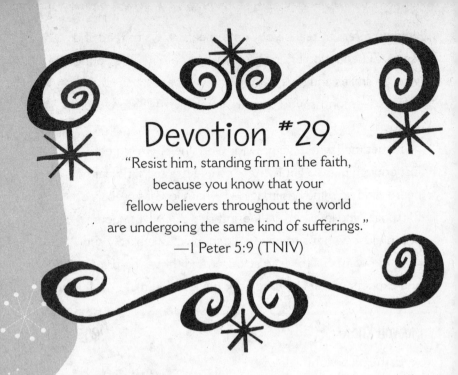

Devotion #29

"Resist him, standing firm in the faith,
because you know that your
fellow believers throughout the world
are undergoing the same kind of sufferings."
—1 Peter 5:9 (TNIV)

In IT Together

Take a stand against the devil's lies when he tests you. Be firm in your faith. Other believers around the world are enduring the same kind of suffering you are. No trial or test has come to you except what is common to everyone. (See 1 Corinthians 10:13.) You are not alone in your suffering.

Abby felt alone though. She felt like her parents just wouldn't let her grow up, and it was embarrassing. She couldn't see the videos other kids saw. Her parents pulled her out of movies shown at school that they considered inappropriate. Her classmates made fun of her for it. Her mom had to okay Abby's clothes before she bought them. That meant popular short-shorts, tight tees, and tiny bathing suits all were left behind in the dressing room. Abby felt like such a baby. She finally let out her frustration in youth group one night. To her amazement, six other girls said they had the exact same frustration! Whether the girls liked it or not, they had godly parents who watched over them. This sometimes brought unfair suffering when the girls got ridiculed at school. When that happens to you, what should be your reaction? "When you do good and suffer, if you take it patiently, this *is* commendable before God" (1 Peter 2:20 NKJV).

No one enjoys being called a baby. Even so, thank the Lord if you have parents willing to help you lead a godly life in an ungodly world. They care about you so much!

Did You Know ...

Job was considered blessed for enduring intense suffering? God knew the good end results he had in mind! (See James 5:11.)

Girl Talk:

When you feel alone, do you share your feelings with anyone, or do you keep things bottled up? What are some ways you can reach out and share your feelings?

More To Explore: 1 Peter 2:21–23

God Talk:

Lord, I know I'm not the only one who suffers trials. Please help me remember that I am not alone. I know you will always love me, and I'm forever grateful. Amen.

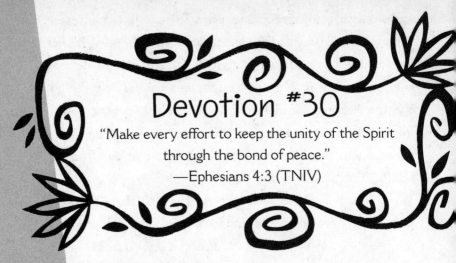

Devotion #30

"Make every effort to keep the unity of the Spirit
through the bond of peace."
—Ephesians 4:3 (TNIV)

Powerful Peace

Have an intense desire to be united to fellow believers. Pursue harmony with others enthusiastically. Peace is powerful. It will keep you stuck together with Holy Spirit superglue! Don't let the devil or another person divide you from other followers. Guard your peace and stay together.

You discover that wanting to be at peace with people and actually doing it are two different things. You truly want to get along with your friends, teachers, and family members. You don't like it when people are upset with you or fighting. Still, you had no idea that staying in harmony would be so hard sometimes. Often, you discover, it involves overlooking some annoying words or actions. Like when your mom barges into your room again without knocking. Or when your best friend forgets it's your birthday. Or when your teacher surprises the class with a quiz over material you forgot to read. Keeping peace and harmony among believers was the apostle Paul's desire too. He wrote, "I appeal to you, brothers and sisters, in the name of our Lord Jesus Christ, that all of you agree with one another in what you say and that there be no divisions among you, but that you be perfectly united in mind and thought" (1 Corinthians 1:10 TNIV). The devil will work overtime to disturb and disrupt this peace, however. He will set you up to get you upset with others. Why? Because Satan knows how powerful people are when they are united in peace. Most things that happen are not worth losing your peace over—nor your power. So stay glued together!

Did You Know ...

the Bible says we believers are all parts of the same body, like eyes and feet are part of the same body? (See 1 Corinthians 12:12–21.) Just like the parts of your body, we all need to work together in harmony.

More To Explore: Romans 14:17–19

Girl Talk:

In what areas of your life do you sense that you're losing your peace? Ask God for help in keeping your peace and staying united with other Christians.

God Talk:

Lord, sometimes it's so hard to live peacefully with everyone. Give me your strength to do this. Amen.

Devotion #31

"Do all things without grumbling
and faultfinding and complaining [against God]
and questioning and doubting [among yourselves]."
—Philippians 2:14 (AMP)

Calm Down—And Cheer Up!

Stay away from complaining and arguing. Grumbling about your life is being discontented with God's will for you. Questioning every little thing isn't helpful either. Don't argue over minor things that don't really matter. Choose to be at peace with God and others.

Taylor didn't like her life anymore. She didn't like having a baby brother and complained about his noise at night. She detested their new neighborhood, which was full of old people. She argued with her mom about babysitting and with her dad about going to the mall alone. Taylor resented the household rules her parents made and questioned everything they asked her to do. One thing really puzzled Taylor though. Her new friend, Amanda, had stricter parents and more brothers than Taylor, yet she was always happy and made others smile too. Nothing seemed to bother her. How did she do it?

Amanda had learned to look for the good things in her life: loving parents, a happy home, good books, and good friends. It's all about attitude (a girl's beliefs and feelings about life). You can choose a rebellious attitude, complaining and arguing about everything. This is what the Bible has to say about rebellious people: "These people are grumblers and fault-finders; they follow their own evil desires; they boast about themselves and flatter others for their own advantage" (Jude v. 16 TNIV). Or you can choose to praise God for his wonderful care, and be thankful for your many blessings. "Let the peace of Christ rule in your hearts, since as members of one body you were called to peace. And be thankful" (Colossians 3:15 TNIV). Choose a thankful attitude—and experience joy and peace.

Did You Know . . .

the word *peace* is mentioned in the Bible 275 times? Sometimes it refers to personal peace with God and within yourself. Other times it refers to peace among people.

More To Explore. James 5:9

Girl Talk:

How would you describe your attitude today? Does it need cleaning up? Find five things you can thank God for right now. Feeling better?

God Talk:

Lord, my attitude stinks sometimes. I'm sorry I'm not always grateful to you for all you've given me. Please help me remember how much I have to be thankful for. Amen.

Devotion #32

"Encourage one another and build each other up,
just as in fact you are doing."
—1 Thessalonians 5:11 (TNIV)

Building Up

As believers, give hope and courage to others going through tough times. Use your words and actions to inspire confidence. Forget about yourself for a while and put your energies into helping others succeed.

You're not usually a quitter, but you feel like quitting now. You've been sick with a viral infection for a month. The infection is about gone, but you're overwhelmed by a month's worth of schoolwork to catch up on. There are two projects to do, whole chapters to read, book reports to write, and tests to take. You can't even decide where to start. You know you'll flunk for sure! Your friend Morgan knocks on the door. "I'm here to help," she says. Sitting down at the table, she makes a "to do" list of each assignment you have to complete. "I know you can do this," Morgan said, "and I'll come over every day after school to help. If we tackle three or four things on the list every day, you'll be caught up in no time." You smile. With your friend's encouragement, you feel like you can succeed!

Some people prefer to tear others down, while others build people up. Some have a special gift for encouraging others, but it's a quality all believers should try to develop. "Let us aim for harmony in the church and try to build each other up" (Romans 14:19 NLT). In practical terms, what does it mean to be an encourager? Speak only those things that are helpful. Study a person's situation. What does that person need? Build them up in that area—and you'll be blessed at the same time.

Did You Know ...

in *Sophie Flakes Out*, Sophie learns that there's a lot of difference between acting grown up and being grown up? Victoria and Ginger seemed older, but their mouths gave away their real lack of maturity.

More To Explore: Hebrews 3:13

Girl Talk:

Who could use your help right now? Think of a few things you could do to help someone, and then volunteer. Whether they accept or not, they'll know you care!

God Talk:

Lord, I know how wonderful it can be to have a friend who helps and encourages. I want to be that friend. Please help me find ways to lift others up.
Thank you. Amen.

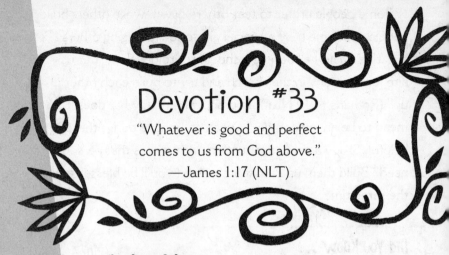

Devotion #33

"Whatever is good and perfect
comes to us from God above."
—James 1:17 (NLT)

Perfect Gifts

God is good and perfect himself, and every good
thing and perfect gift given to us comes from him.
We have all been given good things. Jasmine loves
her new cocker spaniel. Hannah loves making apple
pies with her grandmother. Michelle loves her new baby
sister. Kayla loves having a day off without homework.
Kelsey is grateful for her new jeans. Melissa loves her best
friend's laugh. Amber loves her dad's sense of humor.
Stephanie is grateful for passing her science test. Alexis loves
sitting by the lake on vacation. Each girl is grateful for a different good gift, but each gift ultimately comes from the
same source: God above.

People often think they make their own good
things happen. Far from it. "A person can
receive only what is given from heaven"
(John 3:27 TNIV). Every day we have so
many things to be thankful for, so many
good gifts in our lives. Do we deserve
any of it? No. In fact, even though we
were born sinful, God chose to offer his

very best gift to each of us. "The wages of sin is death, but the gift of God is eternal life in Christ Jesus our Lord" (Romans 6:23 TNIV). When you accept that gift—when Jesus becomes your Savior—it blesses both the giver (God) and the receiver (you)! Every day God showers us with wonderful gifts. What should be our response? "Praise the Lord! Oh, give thanks to the Lord, for He is good!" (Psalm 106:1 NKJV).

Did You Know ...

the book of Psalms is a great place to find ways of saying thanks? David gives thanks to God in at least eleven places. (See, for example, Psalms 18:49; 106:1; and 136:1.)

More To Explore: Matthew 7:11

Girl Talk:

What has God blessed you with lately? Write God a letter right now and thank him.

God Talk:

Lord, you have given me so much. I want to thank you for _____. It means so much to me. You're awesome! Amen.

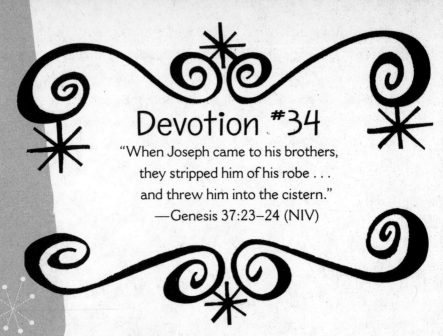

Devotion #34

"When Joseph came to his brothers,
they stripped him of his robe . . .
and threw him into the cistern."
—Genesis 37:23–24 (NIV)

In The Pits

Joseph's father loved him more than his brothers. His father also gave Joseph a beautifully colored robe. Joseph's brothers were so jealous that they ripped off his robe and threw him into a deep, empty well. Later, they sold Joseph as a slave!

Bella also felt other people's jealousy. She had taken voice lessons for years, and she had the best voice in the seventh-grade choir. She was careful not to brag or show off. Although no one was surprised when she won the lead in the spring musical, several girls were angry about it. During one of the rehearsals, a coil of rope was left where Bella would be sure to trip over it. She did—and sprained her ankle so badly that she had to quit the show.

What happened to Bella—and to Joseph—was totally unfair. They may have both asked, "God, why did you let this happen to me?" "Why?" is a question that God often doesn't answer, at least not right away. He asks us to trust him instead, even when bad things happen. Later we may see the good that came out of the bad situation when we trusted God with it. That happened to Joseph. Being sold into slavery in Egypt put Joseph in a position to later save many lives during a widespread famine—including the lives of his brothers. While you wait for God's outcome, he always gives you the power to overcome fear and discouragement.

We don't live in heaven yet. Our world isn't perfect, and neither are people. Sometimes bad things happen. But through it all, always remember: God loves you, and you can trust him. If you're patient, he will bring amazingly good things out of any situation.

Did You Know ...

Sophie and the Corn Flakes had an enemy in *Sophie Tracks a Thief*? Bossy, sarcastic Phoebe was a know-it-all, but Sophie and the other Corn Flakes prayed for her and tried to appreciate her good points.

More To Explore: Romans 8:28

Girl Talk:

Describe the last time you asked God why something happened. Do you trust that God will take care of you no matter what?

God Talk:

Lord, I don't understand why some things happen. Help me to remember that trusting you is the most important thing. Amen.

Mini-Quiz:

Another famous Bible character was thrown unfairly into a pit. Who was it?

a. Job
b. Daniel
c. Esther

Answer: b. Daniel, who was thrown into a pit full of lions!

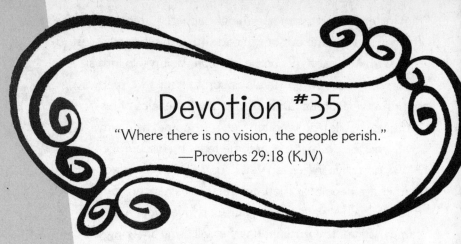

Devotion #35

"Where there is no vision, the people perish."
—Proverbs 29:18 (KJV)

Have a Dream!

People need to have a vision, or goals, for their future. Without God-given goals to guide them, people get off track and totally lose direction for their lives. People of all ages need goals, and God has a plan for each life right now—no matter what your age. Madison had a big vision. From the time she took her first dance lesson at the age of three, she wanted to be a famous ballerina. For nine years she studied and danced. She performed in musicals, at first in the background, but more and more often in lead parts. Madison was well on her way to achieving her dream. Then disaster struck. A drunk driver hit her mom's car and smashed in the passenger side. Madison's left leg was crushed. After three different surgeries, the shattered leg was put back together. She barely limped—but she'd never dance again. Madison sank into depression. Her lifetime goal was gone. Exhausted, she prayed for help daily, but saw no immediate change in her circumstances. However, God's ears were open to her prayers. (See 1 Peter 3:12.)

The next time Madison was at the hospital for physical therapy, she watched a small girl who was learning to walk again. She clapped when the seven-year-old took her first shaky steps. Right then, a new vision was born inside Madison. She'd found a new dream—becoming a physical therapist and helping others walk again. Her depression lifted, and her life was again filled with purpose.

Did You Know ...

even when you make all kinds of plans in your mind, the Lord is the one who really makes the plans work? (See Proverbs 16:9.)

More To Explore: Ezekiel 12:23

Girl Talk:

Have you had to change any goals or dreams? How did you feel about that? Have you asked God what his goals are for you?

God Talk:

Lord, you know I would love to _____. Please show me whether this is your plan for me or not. I want to do what you have in mind for me. Amen.

BEAUTY 101:

Confidence that comes from having a purpose is very beautifying. Confidence shows in your posture, your determination, and your attitude.

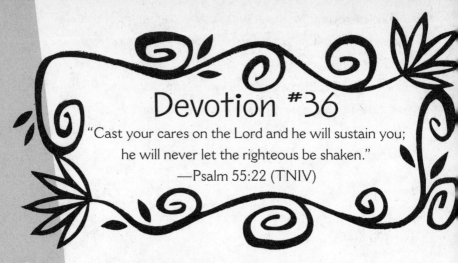

Devotion #36

"Cast your cares on the Lord and he will sustain you;
he will never let the righteous be shaken."
—Psalm 55:22 (TNIV)

Holding Hands

Throw your troubles on the Lord. Let go of them. Release the weight of the worries you carry around. God will take care of you. He won't allow his followers to slip, fall, or fail.

You know about carrying worries and burdens. Your mom is sick with a stomach disorder that keeps her in bed most nights and weekends. She's already missed a lot of work, and the doctor bills are piling up. You help with your little sisters, cook meals, and keep the house clean so your dad can care for your mom. Sometimes, after you wash dishes and put your sisters to bed, you're too tired to tackle your homework. You definitely need the Lord to hold you up and carry your burdens for you.

Worries come in all shapes and sizes, and they can be heavy. Your burden might be divorced parents, hating the way you look, a crabby grandparent who lives with you, money worries, or living in a dangerous neighborhood. Whatever the problem that causes you to stumble, the solution is the same. "The steps of the godly are directed by the Lord. He delights in every detail of their lives. Though they stumble, they will not fall, for the Lord holds them by the hand" (Psalm 37:23–24 NLT). Think of a small child holding on to her daddy's hand. She trips over a rock, but Daddy's hand grips hers tight so she doesn't fall. That's how your heavenly Father holds you. Hold on to God, and let him carry your worries.

Did You Know ...

God might want you to learn something by going *through* a problem or time of suffering? Removing the trouble takes away your chance to learn. God is the potter, and you are the clay being molded into something useful. Sometimes molding hurts! (See Isaiah 64:8.)

More To Explore: 1 Peter 5:7

Girl Talk:

What troubles or worries are getting to you right now? How do you handle them? Have you asked God to hold your hand and get you through it?

God Talk:

Lord, I'm having a hard time with
_____. Please help me get through it and stay strong. I know you can get me through anything. Thank you. Amen.

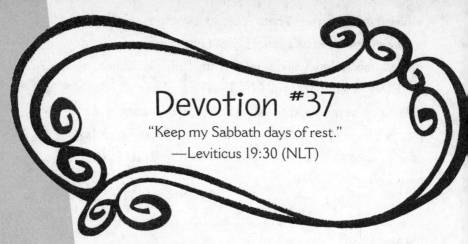

Devotion #37

"Keep my Sabbath days of rest."
—Leviticus 19:30 (NLT)

Take a Break!

Early in Old Testament times, God gave his people the Ten Commandments, or rules for living. One commandment said to rest one day out of every seven. Most believers choose Sunday as their day of rest. It is time to be spent in God's house with other believers, as well as resting time away from work.

Olivia wished she could get some rest. Middle school was harder than she'd expected. Her projects and papers took forever. Add to that practicing her flute, going to gymnastics lessons and piano lessons, babysitting on weekends to make extra money, and youth group—and she felt like she was going to lose it. The commandment to rest one day each week was given for our good. God knew if we didn't get away from our duties to rest, we would simply come apart at the seams. If your mind is focused 24/7 on your schoolwork and activities, you are left with little time to focus on God and his Word. Cut back on activities until you have time to rest one day each week.

Jesus was also concerned about the apostles getting too tired. Once they were so busy that they weren't taking time to rest. "Because so many people were coming and going that they did not even have a chance to eat, he said to them, 'Come with me by yourselves to a quiet place and get some rest'" (Mark 6:31 TNIV). Someone once joked, "Seven days without rest makes one weak." However, it's true. You can't be strong and exhausted at the same time. So follow God's plan, and rest one day a week. If you do, you'll enjoy the other six much more!

Did You Know ...

boys and girls in elementary and middle school need ten to eleven hours of sleep each night? Getting rest during the week is important too! (See Exodus 23:12.)

GirL TaLk:

Make a list of all your activities during one week. Do you have enough time to rest? If not, pray about which activities to cut back on.

God TaLk:

Lord, thank you for giving us a day of rest. Please help me make the best use of my time so that I can actually take a day to rest. Thank you for always wanting what is best for me. Amen.

More To ExpLore: Exodus 20:8; Leviticus 26:2

Devotion #38

"The wise fear the Lord and shun evil,
but a fool is hotheaded and yet feels secure."
—Proverbs 14:16 (TNIV)

Sizzling

People with good sense and judgment respect God and his laws and turn away from evil. A fool is a rebel who goes against God's ways and teachings. Fools rage and carry on in a confident manner. They think no harm will come to them.

You hate going to school and beg your mom to home-school you. You're smart enough, but there's so much fighting near your school. Hotheaded members of rival gangs rage against one another, making the neighborhood danger-ous for everyone. Your biggest fear is getting caught between a couple of warring students on the way home from school. The gang members yell threats and make convincing predictions of what they'll do to one another. You just want to get far away from them and their rage.

Some people believe that respecting God's instructions and avoiding sin will be boring. But it's not boring—it's safe. "The path of the upright leads away from evil; whoever follows that path is safe" (Proverbs 16:17 NLT). Hotheaded, rebellious people can look and sound so confident! "Foolish people claim to know all about the future and tell everyone the details!" (Ecclesiastes 10:14 NLT). But only God knows the outcome of events. "Your own wickedness will punish you. You will see what an evil, bitter thing it is to forsake the Lord your God, having no fear of him. I, the Lord, the Lord Almighty, have spoken!" (Jeremiah 2:19 NLT). Hotheads stir up trouble. A wise person tries to make peace.

Do everything in your power to avoid hotheaded, rebellious people. Your life will be better for it!

Did You Know ...

Samson (a famous Bible hothead) killed many Philistines whenever things did not go well for him? Eventually, his temper landed him in serious trouble. (See Judges 16:20–21.)

More To Explore: Proverbs 3:7

Girl Talk:

Can you describe the last time you dealt with an angry, rebellious person? How could you avoid this person in the future?

God Talk:

Lord, sometimes I can't avoid angry hotheads. At those times, please help me to remain cool and levelheaded and get out of the situation. Thank you for leading me in the right direction. Amen.

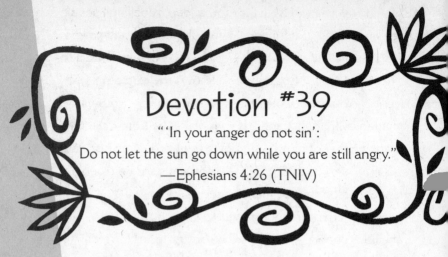

Devotion #39

"'In your anger do not sin':
Do not let the sun go down while you are still angry."
—Ephesians 4:26 (TNIV)

PUT OUT THE FIRE!

Everyone gets angry from time to time. However, when you do get angry, don't handle it in a wrong, sinful way. Don't let your anger control you. Choose to get over it quickly.

Brianna knew about anger. She loaned her new bike to her best friend, who promised to take extra good care of it. It was returned bent and crumpled. Her best friend had left the bike in her driveway, where her dad backed his truck over it. The frame was bent, and the red paint was scratched. Even though her friend offered to get it fixed, Brianna was furious. She wanted to call her friend names and scream at her. Instead she bit her tongue. For an hour, Brianna ranted and raved to herself about her irresponsible friend. When she calmed down, she knew she had a decision to make. Would she punish her friend by venting her anger or giving her the silent treatment? Or would she forgive her and drop it? Brianna called her friend, made arrangements to get the bike fixed, talked about school for a few minutes, then hung up. She still hated that her bike was damaged, but she was glad she'd kept her friend.

Christians don't lose their emotions when they get saved, but you don't have to continue giving in to a bad temper. "Get rid of all bitterness, rage and anger, brawling and slander, along with every form of malice" (Ephesians 4:31 TNIV). Don't just stop there. After dealing with your anger, take things one step further: "Clothe yourselves with compassion, kindness, humility, gentleness and patience" (Colossians 3:12 TNIV). Ask God to change you from the inside out. He will!

Did You Know ...

even Jesus showed fury at times? For example, with a whip made of cords, he drove the money changers and those selling animals for sacrifice out of the temple! He said they had made his temple into a den of robbers. (See Matthew 21:12–13.)

More To Explore: Proverbs 14:29

Girl Talk:

Has anger ever gotten the best of you? What could you have done instead of giving in to your anger?

God Talk:

Lord, I know I don't always handle anger well. Please help me not to give in to my anger. I want to stay calm and forgiving, like you. Amen.

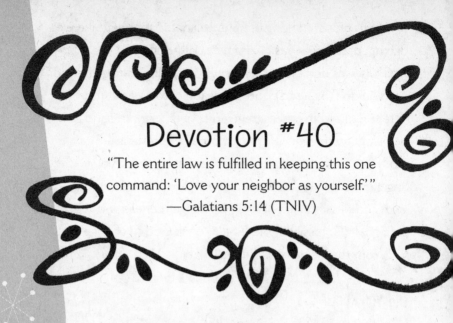

Devotion #40

"The entire law is fulfilled in keeping this one
command: 'Love your neighbor as yourself.'"
—Galatians 5:14 (TNIV)

Spread The Love Around

In the Old and New Testaments, there are many laws
and commands about how we are to treat one another.
However, they can all be summed up in one easy-to-
remember idea: Love the people around you just as you love
yourself.

You may find that loving your neighbor isn't as easy as it
sounds. You've always liked your neighbors, but then one summer the Carlsons move in next door. With the noise blaring
from their house, you figure they have at least a dozen kids
and six dogs. It turns out to be only five small children and
two dogs, but you think it's still too many. Your bedroom windows overlook the Carlson house, and
you hate having your windows open now.

You no longer hear the breeze blowing
through the pines or meadowlarks chirp-
ing. Instead, noise and commotion—kids
yelling and dogs barking—blast from the
house next door till long after you go to bed.

Loving these new neighbors will take a lot of work, you decide.

First, you need a change of heart. "Do not . . . bear a grudge against anyone among your people, but love your neighbor as yourself. I am the Lord" (Leviticus 19:18 TNIV). And "Let all bitterness, wrath, anger, clamor, and evil speaking be put away from you, with all malice. And be kind to one another, tenderhearted, forgiving one another, even as God in Christ forgave you" (Ephesians 4:31–32 NKJV). Over the next week, you work out a strategy. Twice you offer to babysit the kids, you accompany the older ones to the neighborhood pool, and you take them all to your church's vacation Bible school for a week. Through these acts of service, you actually grow to enjoy your new neighbors.

Did You Know . . .

"loving your neighbor as yourself" includes any strangers who might be visiting you? (See Leviticus 19:34.)

More To Explore: Romans 13:8–10

Girl Talk:

How do you treat those around you? Does your heart match your actions? What is one thing you can do for a neighbor today?

God Talk:

Lord, sometimes it's hard to love everyone around me. Please change my attitude. I want to be as kind and loving as you. Thank you. Amen.

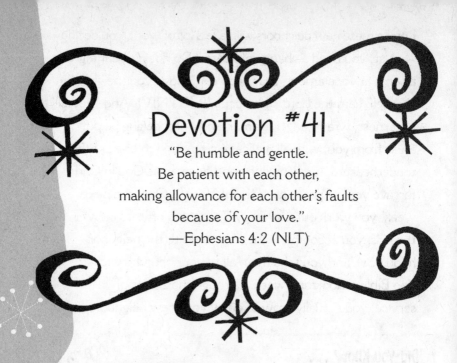

Devotion #41

"Be humble and gentle.
Be patient with each other,
making allowance for each other's faults
because of your love."
—Ephesians 4:2 (NLT)

God's Kind of Allowance

Live in a way that shows you're a follower of Jesus. How does Jesus act? He's unselfish, gentle, and mild. He shows patience and is understanding about our failures and weaknesses. We should love one another in the same way.

Kelsey heard an inspiring sermon about loving others the way Jesus loved her. All aglow with warm feelings, she was determined to show God's love to each person she met.

Before the day was over, she realized she didn't always want to love others. She loved helping people who were nice to her, like her mom and older sister. It irritated her to be gentle or humble with her older brother, who thought he ruled the world and everyone in it. She was patient with her elderly neighbor, who was hard of hearing. But tolerating her best friend's bad memory when she forgot to pick up Kelsey for the movie was something else. Slowly it dawned on Kelsey that we are told to love others—*period*. Having warm, fuzzy feelings has nothing to do it.

What are some actions you can take to love others better? For one thing, don't give up on people when they mess up. Make allowances instead. "[Love] always protects, always trusts, always hopes, always perseveres" (1 Corinthians 13:7 TNIV). Also come alongside people in trouble and help them through it. Everyone has a crisis from time to time. A loving person helps shoulder the load until the crisis passes. "Carry each other's burdens, and in this way you will fulfill the law of Christ" (Galatians 6:2 TNIV). Remember how much God loves you—then share that love with others.

Did You Know . . .

Joseph had every reason to hate his brothers, but didn't? They sold him into slavery, but he saved their lives from famine years later. (See Genesis 47:5–12.) That's loving others no matter what!

More To Explore: Romans 15:1

Girl Talk:

Is there anyone whose behavior is irritating you right now? How can you show love to that individual instead of impatience?

God Talk:

Lord, I know I need to love everyone, but I'm having a hard time with _____. Please give me the right words as I try to show this person love. Thank you. Amen.

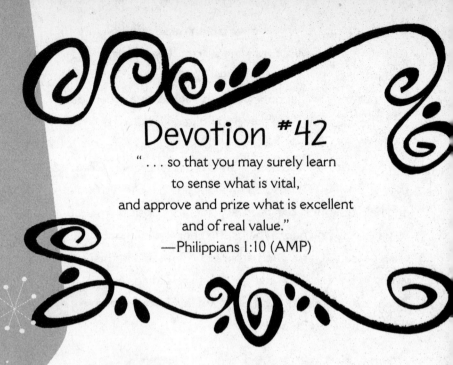

Devotion #42

" . . . so that you may surely learn
to sense what is vital,
and approve and prize what is excellent
and of real value."
—Philippians 1:10 (AMP)

True Value

Every day we make choices: what TV shows and movies to watch, what music to listen to, what words to say. Learn to treasure things of excellence. Don't copy the standards of the world. Go deeper. Value what really counts.

When Jessica moved to a new town and started middle school, she studied the various groups of girls. Who would be her new friends? Only a couple of people from her new Sunday school class attended her middle school. She liked both Teri and Elizabeth—they were fun and kind and friendly—but they definitely weren't "cool." On the other hand, Brit and Kayla were obviously the most popular girls. Boys swarmed around them. They invited Jessica to sit at their lunch table, and, at first, Jessica was thrilled to be singled out. But the filthy language she heard there—and the nasty backbiting of other students—made her feel dirty. Jessica had a choice to make. Would she choose friends of excellent moral value with high standards? Or would she settle for friends with glitz but no character?

How can you learn to prize what God values? Read God's Word and let it change your thinking. "Do not conform to the pattern of this world, but be transformed by the renewing of your mind. Then you will be able to test and approve what God's will is—his good, pleasing and perfect will" (Romans 12:2 TNIV). Choosing what God values will place you in the center of his will—and there's no better place on earth to be!

Did You Know ...

Sodom and Gomorrah's standards were so worldly that God could not find even ten righteous people in those cities? He destroyed the cities with burning sulfur. (See Genesis 19:24.)

More To Explore: I Thessalonians 5:21

Girl Talk:

What do you suppose God thinks about the decisions you make and the people you hang out with? If there's room for improvement, ask God for help in making better decisions.

God Talk:

Lord, I don't always make the best choice with my time. In everything I do, I want you to be proud of me. Please help me make the right decisions. Amen.

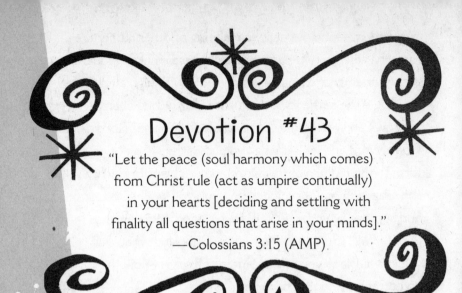

Devotion #43

"Let the peace (soul harmony which comes)
from Christ rule (act as umpire continually)
in your hearts [deciding and settling with
finality all questions that arise in your minds]."
—Colossians 3:15 (AMP)

Strike Three—You're Out!

Pray about decisions. Then let God's peace be the deciding factor in whether you go ahead with something or not. You must pray for direction and allow God time and opportunity to respond. Don't fake it, claiming you have God's peace about a decision when it's just your own desire to do something.

Let's say you need to make a decision. You want to go out for volleyball, your mom suggests that you sign up for flute lessons, and your dad thinks you might start an after-school babysitting business instead. It's your choice. You wish you could do all three, but there isn't enough time. You have to choose, but you're so confused! God's Word doesn't specifically tell you which activity to pursue. Your parents have different opinions, but leave the choice up to you. You pray quickly about it, but may stay confused if you don't take time to listen.

Don't blindly push ahead with a plan until you feel at peace. Sit or lie down at night, be still, and pray about your situation. Is there any anxiety in your heart? Do you think of reasons this might be a bad idea? Does your conscience warn you that there's something wrong in your plan of action? If you sense any of these things, stop. Don't make that decision yet. It might not be God's will, or it just might not be the right time yet. You might sense a "no" answer or a "not yet" answer. Even if that's frustrating, don't push ahead. "Trust in the Lord with all your heart; do not depend on your own understanding. Seek his will in all you do, and he will direct your paths" (Proverbs 3:5–6 NLT). Wait for God to guide where it's safe to follow.

Did You Know ...

a good place to start is to make a list of positives and negatives of the decision you need to make? This can give you a better idea of what to pray about.

More To Explore: James 1:5

Girl Talk:

Do you have a question for God right now? What would you like to know? Ask him for help, then be quiet and wait for an answer. He will tell you!

God Talk:

Lord, please help me be quiet and wait for your guidance. I want to be certain I'm doing your will. Thank you. Amen.

Devotion #44

"God tested Abraham's faith and obedience."
—Genesis 22:1 (NLT)

This Is Only a Test

Sometimes God tests us to strengthen our faith or prove our loyalty. Only a test will reveal if we truly mean what we say. Abraham had already passed many tests, but none as big as when God asked him to sacrifice his only son, Isaac. God needed to see if Abraham would be obedient no matter what God asked him to do.

God tests people today too. Things are tight financially at your house after your dad loses his job. Your friends want to go to the movies Friday night, but you can't ask your parents for the money. They're barely able to pay the rent. That day when you stop at a convenience store on the way home, you find a wallet someone dropped. A twenty-dollar bill is inside. An answer to your prayers! Or is it? You know it's wrong to steal. (See Exodus 20:15.)

The money belongs to the man whose name is on the driver's license in the wallet. Sighing, you turn in the wallet to the cashier. You pass the test! You learn that you have an honest character.

Do you face a test today? What can you learn from this lesson that might help you in the weeks and years to come? Think of one test you're facing—a grumpy teacher, a difficult parent, an annoying little sister? How might God use that test to prepare you for tomorrow?

"The refining pot *is* for silver and the furnace for gold, but the Lord tests the hearts" (Proverbs 17:3 NKJV). Silver and gold are made pure in the fire. Heat removes the worthless material (the impurities). People are refined in God's fire of testing for the same reason. When your next test comes, pray and ask for God's help, then pass the test with flying colors!

Did You Know ...

Abraham was obedient when God asked him to sacrifice his only son? Read Genesis 22 to discover what happens.

More To Explore: Exodus 16:4

Girl Talk:

Do you think God is testing you on something? How do you think he wants you to respond?

God Talk:

Lord, I want to pass any test that you give me. Help me to please you. Amen.

BEAUTY 101

The night before a test, get eight hours of beauty rest. Not only will you look better, you'll concentrate better and remember the material you studied.

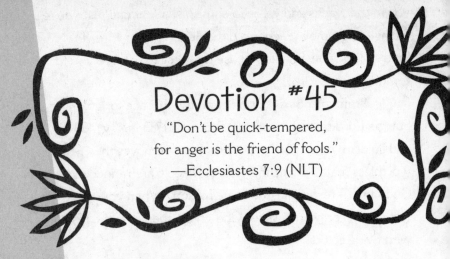

Devotion #45

"Don't be quick-tempered,
for anger is the friend of fools."
—Ecclesiastes 7:9 (NLT)

COOL IT!

Anger is a strong emotion. It's usually directed at someone we believe has wronged us. A quick-tempered person gets angry easily and lets that anger control her actions and words. "The quick-tempered do foolish things" (Proverbs 14:17 TNIV). Grace didn't mean to have a quick temper. In fact, her instant reactions even took her by surprise sometimes. She was careful at school and never lost her cool with teachers or friends. But at home, everyone irritated her. Her mom gave too many directions. Her dad bugged her to get off the phone and study. Her older brother was bossy, and her little brother swiped her stuff. *Who wouldn't get angry?* she reasoned. Grace reacted quickly, spouting what was on her mind—and landed in hot water. She gave her mom and dad lip— and was grounded. (Then she had to explain to her friends why she had to miss the weekend birthday party.) She smarted off to her big brother—and he left for the mall without her. (She had to explain to her teacher why she still didn't have the right note-book for her project.) She screamed at her little brother—and he went bawling to her parents. (Grace was then assigned dishwashing chores for a week.)

Finally she was tired of the consequences for displaying her quick temper. Sighing, she read the verses her mom had marked in her Bible to read. One in particular struck her as sensible: "Everyone should be quick to listen, slow to speak and slow to become angry, because our anger does not produce the righteousness that God desires" (James 1:19–20 TNIV). Grace prayed for help, knowing she had a hard road ahead of her. But she really wanted to con-quer her temper—and she knew that with God's help, she could do it.

Did You Know ...

we are supposed to get over our anger before the sun goes down? (See Ephesians 4:26.)

Girl Talk:

When was the last time you lost your cool? How do you feel about what you said and did? Do you have to work at keep-ing your temper under control?

More To Explore: Proverbs 16:32

God Talk:

Lord, sometimes I don't think before I speak. When I get angry, it's hard to keep quiet. Please help me control my temper. Thank you.
    Amen.

Devotion #46

"All the people took off their earrings and brought
them to Aaron. He took what they handed him and
made it into an idol cast in the shape of a calf,
fashioning it with a tool . . .
'Then they gave me the gold, and I threw it
into the fire, and out came this calf!'"
—Exodus 32:3–4, 24 (TNIV)

Owning Up

When Moses was up on the mountain with God, the impatient Israelites asked Aaron (Moses' brother) to make them an idol. Aaron collected their gold jewelry and made a golden calf for them to worship instead of God. When Moses returned and saw them worshipping the golden calf, he was furious. Aaron quickly explained that he couldn't help it. Somehow, when he threw the gold into the fire, a calf popped out! He spoke as if he'd had nothing to do with it.

We're all tempted to lie when we get caught. Maybe you babysit your little brother Jake on Saturday while your parents work. While he watches cartoons, you close your eyes for a minute.

An hour later you wake up to an empty room and a blaring TV. There's no Jake to be found. Running outside, you spot him at the picnic table, arranging flowers. "Oh, no!" you whisper. Jake has picked every one of your mother's prize roses and is making bouquets from them. Later, when confronted by your mom, you say that you were outside with Jake, ran indoors when the phone rang, and by the time you got back outside, he'd cut all the flowers. Mom doesn't buy it, and you feel guilty.

"The Lord detests lying lips" (Proverbs 12:22 TNIV). So the next time you do something wrong, confess it instead of covering up. Apologize. Make things right if you can. Then put it behind you and move on.

Did You Know ...

King Solomon once figured out who was a liar by giving an order to cut a baby in half? Read 1 Kings 3:16–28.

More To Explore: Genesis 3:12–13

Girl Talk:

Think of the last time you were tempted to lie. What did you decide to do? Is it what God would have wanted you to do?

God Talk:

Lord, sometimes it is so tempting to lie. Please help me to remember that my lying hurts others and breaks your heart, and that nothing good can come from deception. Thank you for always being with me. Amen.

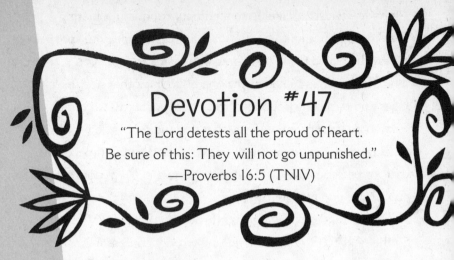

Devotion #47

"The Lord detests all the proud of heart.
Be sure of this: They will not go unpunished."
—Proverbs 16:5 (TNIV)

Ain'T I Grand?

God intensely dislikes people full of pride. They may believe they're hot stuff and in control of everything. However, punishment and consequences will cause their downfall.

Alyssa had no idea she was puffy with pride. She was just excited when her teacher decided to publish a two-page weekly classroom newspaper. Alyssa loved to write stories, she always got As in English, and she knew she was the best choice for editor. Alyssa wanted the newspaper done right. She told the teacher that she was the best person to be in charge. When Kylie was chosen as editor instead, Alyssa demanded to know why. Mr. Jackson shrugged. "Kylie's grades aren't as high as yours, but she works better with people. She listens to them." In other words, Kylie wasn't too proud to consider her classmates' ideas.

God despises the proud, overly self-confident person. "He mocks proud mockers but shows favor to the humble and oppressed" (Proverbs 3:34 TNIV).

Why is pride such a big deal? A haughty, stuck-up person finds it impossible to be kind, gentle, or forgiving. Pride also causes us to think we can run our own lives without God's help. Even the devil—who started out as an angel in heaven—let pride ruin his life. (When he decided he wanted to be God himself, Satan was thrown out of heaven forever.) So does being humble mean you will crawl on the ground like a worm all your life? Absolutely not! "When you bow down before the Lord and admit your dependence on him, he will lift you up and give you honor" (James 4:10 NLT). Be humble—and let God raise you up in his time.

Did You Know ...

there's a whole novel about pride? In *Pride and Prejudice* by Jane Austen, pride almost costs the main character her whole future.

More To Explore: Proverbs 11:2

Girl Talk:

Can you describe a time you felt really confident about something, only to have it blow up in your face? What do you think God was trying to tell you?

God Talk:

Lord, sometimes I get so confident about something, I forget to ask you if it's the right thing for me to do. Help me stay close to you and keep my ego in perspective. Amen.

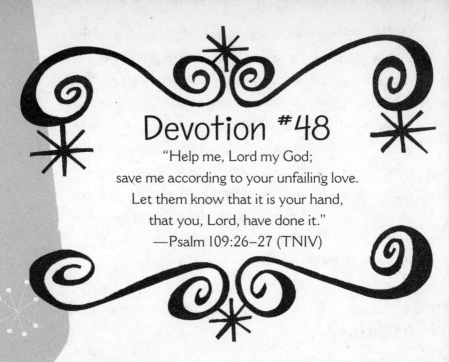

Devotion #48

"Help me, Lord my God;
save me according to your unfailing love.
Let them know that it is your hand,
that you, Lord, have done it."
—Psalm 109:26–27 (TNIV)

Who Did It?

When you need help, cry out to God. He loves you more than you could ever measure. God will rescue you in such a way that it's clear to others who did it.

Your family is having some tough times since your dad lost his job. It's hard just paying the rent and buying groceries. When the overnight class trip to the state park is announced, your heart sinks. The whole trip costs "only" $65, but you know it might as well be a million. You can't ask your parents for it. You don't want to see the embarrassment and hurt on their faces when they have to turn you down. Instead, you pray: "Lord, you know I'd love to go on this trip with my class. Could you show me a way? Please give me money for the trip."

You know that if God wants you to go, he can make a way. Even so, when the answer comes, it astounds you. Your painting for the local art show wins first place, and someone offers to buy it—for $75! When your friends say, "Man, are you lucky!" you don't just smile and agree. "It isn't luck," you say. "I prayed for money to go on the trip, and God did it for me." You give God the credit. "Our mouths were filled with laughter, our tongues with songs of joy. Then it was said among the nations, 'The Lord has done great things for them'" (Psalm 126:2 TNIV). Pray for help, thank the Lord for his answers—and remember to tell others who made it happen!

Did You Know ...

God used his power to change dry lands into flourishing gardens and ruined towns into fortified cities where people could live? (See Ezekiel 36:33–36.)

Girl Talk:

Describe an impossible situation that worked out just in time. Who or what did you give the credit to?

More To Explore: Genesis 21:1–6

God Talk:

Lord, I know nothing is impossible with you. Please help me with _____. I know if you want it, it will happen. Thank you. Amen.

Devotion #49

"Children, obey your parents in the Lord,
for this is right. 'Honor your father and mother'—
which is the first commandment with a promise—
'so that it may go well with you and that
you may enjoy long life on the earth.'"
—Ephesians 6:1–3 (TNIV)

Honoring Parents

There are many commandments, but the first one with a
promise attached is aimed at kids. Children are to honor their
fathers and mothers. That means to show respect and obey
them. And the promise? That you'll live a long and successful
life.

Sophia's mom died when she was only five years old,
and when Sophia was eight, her dad remarried. Sophia
liked Susan, her stepmother, except when she told
her to do her homework or wash supper dishes.
"You're not my real mom," Sophia said, "so
you can't tell me what to do." When she
complained to her best friend, Taylor,
about it, Taylor only laughed. "You
wouldn't like washing dishes even if
Susan was your real mom." Sophia

admitted Taylor was right. Even if her real mom were still alive, she wouldn't want to do her homework or chores.

It's not about whether you like doing what your parents ask. It's about being obedient because you love God. What if you have a cranky parent who is hard to please? What if they rarely say "thank you" or give you encouraging words? Does God still want you to obey parents like this? Yes. Your parents' attitude has nothing to do with it. It might seem unfair, but the Lord is pleased when you're obedient in everything, no matter what. It's certainly *easier* to obey anyone—parent, teacher, boss—who is kind and encouraging. But you can trust God to give you the strength to obey those in authority over you, no matter how they act. God will richly reward you for obeying when it's hard.

Did You Know ...

keeping a positive attitude is one of the best skills you can develop? The way you approach things and how you respond to them will take you farther than any college degree. (See Philippians 4:8.)

More To Explore: Proverbs 6:20–22

Girl Talk:

How easy is it for you to obey your parents? Is there anything about your attitude that should change?

God Talk:

Lord, I know you want me to obey and respect my mom and dad. Please help me keep the right attitude toward them. Amen.

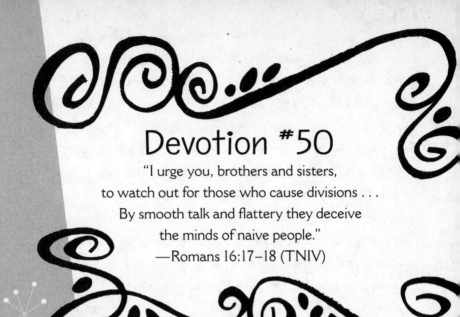

Devotion #50

"I urge you, brothers and sisters,
to watch out for those who cause divisions . . .
By smooth talk and flattery they deceive
the minds of naive people."
—Romans 16:17–18 (TNIV)

Fooled by Flattery

Pay attention to people whose words cause trouble or
divide friends. Their slick words are easily swallowed, but
their glowing comments fool innocent, unsuspecting people.

You have been best friends with Sara for three years, but
when Britney moves in next door to you, things change.
Every time Sara calls you, Britney is there. Britney now
rides to school with you too. You wish you could be best
friends with them both. Britney is so sophisticated, and
she thinks you're the cutest girl in your class. She
also gushes about your parents being cool,
your house being neat, and your baby
brother being adorable. Soon Britney is
running in and out of your house as if it
were her own. However, a month later
things began to disappear from your
home: your dad's watch, money from

your mom's purse, a DVD. You are horrified to realize that things turn up missing after Britney has visited. You were so flattered by Britney's praise that you didn't see the real reason behind it.

Unfortunately, there are some phony people in the world. Like Britney, such people are looking for people to use. "These people . . . boast about themselves and flatter others for their own advantage" (Jude v. 16 TNIV). Sincere compliments from a friend are wonderful! But wise up—and don't be fooled by phony flattery.

Did You Know . . .

people who flatter with their tongues are said to have a throat that's an open grave? Gruesome! (See Psalm 5:9.)

Girl Talk:

Have you ever been tricked by someone you know? How did you feel? Are you more cautious now?

More To Explore: Colossians 2:4

God Talk:

Lord, I feel so mad and used when I get tricked. Help me forgive those who fool me. Please help me pick people who aren't phonies. Thank you. Amen.

Mini-Quiz:

Who is the phony?

a. Steph started an algebra study group to help other students with their math. To thank her, they gave her a pizza party.

b. Maggie befriends other girls with lots of compliments. Then she invites herself over for dinner two or three nights a week.

Answer: b. Maggie

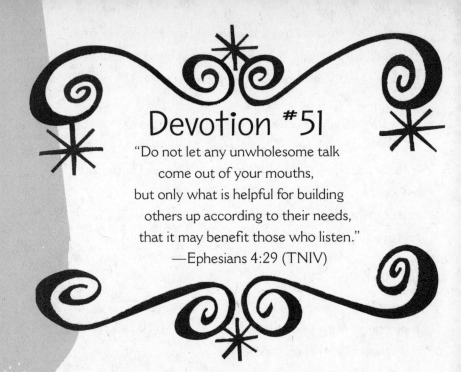

Devotion #51

"Do not let any unwholesome talk
come out of your mouths,
but only what is helpful for building
others up according to their needs,
that it may benefit those who listen."
—Ephesians 4:29 (TNIV)

Power-Packed Words

Believers shouldn't use foul or abusive language. Instead, let everything you say be good and helpful, so that your words will be an encouragement to those who hear them. Words are powerful. Use them to build others up—not tear them down.

Morgan's mom used words as weapons, and Morgan often felt the sting. Sometimes she was called stupid or lazy. At other times, her mom made nasty predictions about her. "You'll never amount to anything," her mom said, "and I knew it from the moment you were born." But Morgan made two decisions: (1) With God's help, she wouldn't be like her mom. She'd learn to speak kind words and be encouraging. (2) She'd concentrate on her teacher's words instead: "You have such a lovely smile, Morgan." "You worked very hard on this lesson, Morgan." "I look forward to seeing you every day, Morgan." Morgan soaked in her teacher's kindness.

"The tongue has the power of life and death" (Proverbs 18:21 TNIV). Morgan decided to "choose life" by taking in the life-giving words of her teacher and trying to be like her. Remember, "Gentle words bring life and health" (Proverbs 15:4 NLT). You—and you alone—control what comes out of your mouth. Choose your words to bless others.

Did You Know ...

in James 3:4–8, the tongue is compared to the rudder of a great ship? The rudder is very small, but it can turn the whole ship. One small tongue can determine the direction of a whole life.

More To Explore: Proverbs 10:32

Girl Talk:

How often in the past few days have nasty words escaped your lips? What could you have said instead in those situations? Remember, silence is also an option!

God Talk:

Lord, pleasant words don't always come out of my mouth. Please help me remember to think before I speak. I want to build others up, not tear them down. Thank you. Amen.

Fun Factoid

More comparisons of the tongue:
- a sharpened razor (See Psalm 52:2.)
- a club or a sword (See Proverbs 25:18.)
- an arrow (See Jeremiah 9:8.)

Devotion #52

"Peace I leave with you;
My [own] peace I now give and bequeath to you.
Not as the world gives do I give to you.
Do not let your hearts be troubled,
neither let them be afraid.
[Stop allowing yourselves to be agitated and disturbed;
and do not permit yourselves to be fearful
and intimidated and cowardly and unsettled.]"
—John 14:27 AMP)

Settle Down!

Jesus gives his followers a gift that is priceless: his peace. The world's peace can evaporate the minute circumstances turn negative. On the other hand, Jesus' peace is total well-being and inner rest of spirit. The peace Jesus gives is solid. It should be, since the Lord is the Rock! (See Psalm 18:46.)

Maybe you need that kind of peace. You pace back and forth across the living room, muttering under your breath. You can't believe it. Both your best friends have been chosen for pep squad, but not you! Your cheers at tryouts were just as good as theirs! Why weren't you chosen?

Weren't you pretty enough? Did you look awkward or stupid? The more you fume, the worse you feel. Not being chosen for pep squad is disappointing—but you're allowing yourself to get emotionally troubled by keeping your mind stirred up. Two hours later, when you have a headache and an upset stomach, you decide to get a grip. You pour your heart out to God, giving him your frustration and disappointment—and fear that your friends will now leave you behind. You let it go and allow Jesus' peace to fill your heart, calm your emotions, and settle your thoughts.

Yes, it's disappointing. But tryouts are over, and you still have all the good things in your life that you had before. God is in control, and he knows more about the situation than you do. Remember, "The Lord will give strength to His people; the Lord will bless His people with peace" (Psalm 29:11 NKJV).

Did You Know ...

the peace symbol was originally the logo for the Campaign for Nuclear Disarmament? Gerald Holtom designed it in 1958, as part of an antinuclear protest march in Britain.

More To Explore: John 16:33

Girl Talk:

Have you had any disappointments lately? How did you deal with them? Have you tried asking Jesus to give you his peace?

God Talk:

Lord, I know things won't always go my way. Please give me your peace about each situation. Thank you for always being with me. Amen.

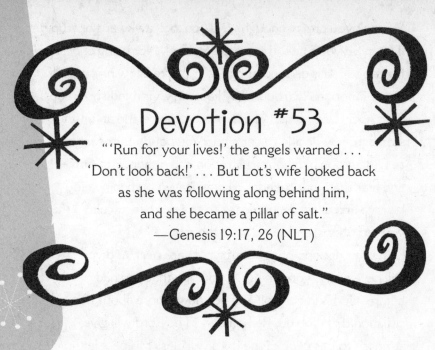

Devotion #53

"'Run for your lives!' the angels warned . . .
'Don't look back!' . . . But Lot's wife looked back
as she was following along behind him,
and she became a pillar of salt."
—Genesis 19:17, 26 (NLT)

No Looking Back

The city of Sodom, where Lot lived, was very wicked. Before God destroyed it, he sent angels to warn Lot and his family to run to the mountains for safety. They were instructed not to look back at their old way of life.

Natalie had to walk away from something too. Her best friend took cigarettes from her mom's purse, lit up, and offered one to Natalie. She didn't want it, but she didn't want her friend to think she was a baby. Within a month, Natalie was hooked. Her hands shook and she got headaches if she went too long without smoking. Finally, she decided she hated the smell, the taste, the cost, the sneaking around, and the headaches. It was hard, but she quit. Her best friend still offered her cigarettes, but Natalie walked away from the habit and didn't look back.

The angels warned Lot's family to run from the city and not look back. Lot's wife ignored that warning and paid with her life. What's wrong with looking back on a past you want to escape? It usually means you have a divided heart. You want to do God's will, but part of you wants to keep your old habits. You can't live with one foot in the world and one foot in God's kingdom and be happy. When you decide to leave a sinful habit behind, make a clean break. Face forward. Don't look back and take a chance of being trapped again. It's not worth it!

Did You Know ...

breaking a habit takes at least twenty-one days? Take time to begin healthy behaviors to replace the bad ones so you can actually break the habit.

More To Explore: Luke 17:31-32

Girl Talk:

Do you have a sinful habit or something that you want to put in your past? How can God help you break away from it?

God Talk:

Lord, you know that I struggle with _____. Please help me put it in the past and leave it there. I want to concentrate on you. Amen.

Fun Factoid

Even today, grotesque salt formations near the southern end of the Dead Sea are reminders of Lot's wife's foolishness.

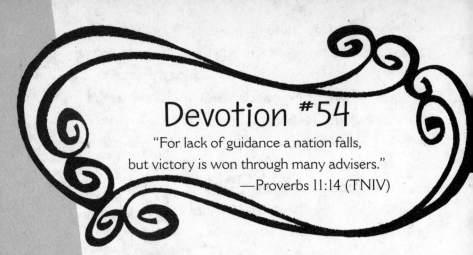

Devotion #54

"For lack of guidance a nation falls,
but victory is won through many advisers."
—Proverbs 11:14 (TNIV)

Listen Up!

We all go through struggles in life. There are many tests along the way, and believers should be able to pass those tests successfully. Failure often comes, however, because we keep our problems a secret instead of asking for help. There can be successful endings to our struggles and tests if we seek guidance from several counselors and advisers.

One day you notice a dark spot on your shoulder. How did you manage to get ink or marker there? You scrub till the skin is pink, but the spot remains. You forget about it, but a month later, you notice it again. It seems darker—and bigger. You scrub till it bleeds and cover it with a Band-Aid. Then one day you read an article in a teen magazine about skin cancer. It says to watch out for moles that darken or grow. You pray about it and go to talk to your mom. "Look at this," you say, peeling off the Band-Aid. After consulting a dermatologist (skin doctor), you have the suspicious mole removed. It isn't skin cancer—not yet. But getting advice from your mom and the skin doctor may have saved your life. Ignoring the problem could have been deadly.

When you have a problem, it's good to share it with trusted others, like a parent, teacher, counselor, youth pastor, or doctor. Confiding in your best friend is fine, but your friend may not know what to do either. "Plans fail for lack of counsel, but with many advisers they succeed" (Proverbs 15:22 TNIV). It can be scary to share your problem with an adult, but it's even scarier keeping it to yourself and not knowing what to do. People care about you and want to help. Let them!

Did You Know ...

even King Jehoshaphat consulted with his people before making some decisions? (See 2 Chronicles 20:21.)

Girl Talk:

Is there anything you are worried about right now? Can you name one or two adults you trust who could help you out? God is always there for guidance too!

God Talk:

Lord, I'm worried about _____. Please help me know who I should talk with about this. I don't want to worry about it anymore. Amen.

More To Explore: Proverbs 24:6

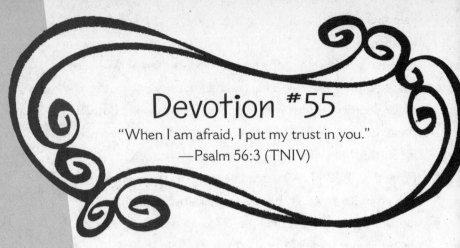

Devotion #55

"When I am afraid, I put my trust in you."
—Psalm 56:3 (TNIV)

I Will Not Fear

When you're afraid, turn to God and pray. Have confidence in the Lord, and put your faith in him. You can count on him for help. If you concentrate on how much the Lord can be trusted, your fears will slip away.

Chloe was afraid all the time. Her single mom had lost her job, and she was often sick. Her dad moved clear across the country. Chloe was being bullied at school by three tough girls who followed her around. She kept quiet about it, not wanting to add to her mother's worries. No matter where she turned—at school or at home—there was something for Chloe to fear. Then Amber invited Chloe to church.

Chloe learned about trusting in Jesus as her Savior, and how everything was under God's control. Now she didn't have to fight her fears alone. She could trust God to work, free her from fear, and deal with the scary situations. Sometimes, believers even brood about their fears. They forget something very important—connecting with God through prayer. "I prayed to the

Lord, and he answered me, freeing me from all my fears" (Psalm 34:4 NLT). Talk to the Lord. Tell him your worries and concerns. Thank him that he has everything under control—even the things that look out-of-control to you. Sometimes fears can make you feel lonely and cut off from God. What if you've prayed, but you feel like your prayers aren't reaching heaven? Our emotions are poor judges of the truth. You may not feel God's help, but keep on praying. Freedom from your fears will come. "In sudden fear I had cried out, 'I have been cut off from the Lord!' But you heard my cry for mercy and answered my call for help" (Psalm 31:22 NLT).

Did You Know ...

when Paul first went into Macedonia, he and fellow Christians were plagued and exhausted by conflicts and fears? God comforted them by sending Titus. Read 2 Corinthians 7:5–7.

More To Explore: 2 Chronicles 20:3

Girl Talk:

How often do you pray when you're afraid? What do you rely on to help you through fear?

God Talk:

Lord, I know you can take away all my fears. Please help me to hold on to you and wait for your help. Amen.

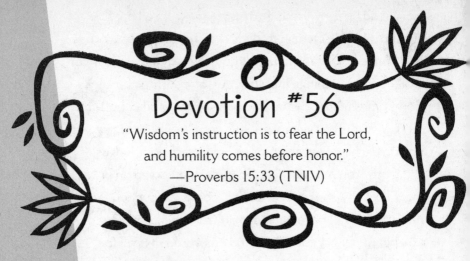

Devotion #56

"Wisdom's instruction is to fear the Lord,
and humility comes before honor."
—Proverbs 15:33 (TNIV)

Deal With It!

Fearing the Lord—deeply respecting him—
teaches a person to be wise. Part of that wisdom is
learning humility. Being humble and modest comes
before God rewards and honors you.

You know you're a talented artist. However, when your
social studies group meets to discuss your group project,
you keep quiet. On the other hand, Kenna boasts how artis-
tic she is, saying, "I'll do all the artwork for our presentation
myself." Kenna doesn't want any suggestions. But on Monday
when the group members see her posters, the disappointment is obvious. Finally Morgan says, "Since we all get the
same group grade, I want Elizabeth to do the posters
instead. She does the neatest drawings in art
class." They vote, and despite Kenna's pout-
ing, they ask you to redo the art.

In our competitive world, people often
think humility (putting others first) is a
weakness. Nothing could be further
from the truth. It takes strength of character to be humble. Exactly how do you

humble yourself? Make others more important—in both attitude and action. For example, if certain possessions cause you pride, give them away (secretly). If you get a big head about your appearance, compliment others on their good features. If you're proud of all your knowledge, make yourself be quiet and let others speak. If you're stuck-up about a special talent you have, find someone less talented and help them achieve! Deal with your "I'm-so-hot" attitude so God doesn't have to do it for you. "Humble yourselves under the mighty power of God, and in his good time he will honor you" (1 Peter 5:6 NLT). When God knows the time is right—when giving you honor won't give you a swelled head—he will reward you.

Did You Know . . .

the Lord actually *hates* "I'm-so-hot" pride and calls it evil? (See Proverbs 8:13.)

God Talk:

Lord, I thank you for giving me talents. Please help me rely on you for any honor you see fit to give me. Thank you. Amen.

More To Explore: Proverbs 18:12

Girl Talk:

What area in your life gives you a swelled head? Think of a few simple steps to humble yourself and compliment others in this area.

Devotion #57

"Insults and reproach have broken my heart;
I am full of heaviness and I am distressingly sick.
I looked for pity, but there was none,
and for comforters, but I found none."
—Psalm 69:20 (AMP)

Sticks and Stones

Insults, shameful comments, criticisms—all are words intended to hurt you. If you have a verbal abuser in your home, school, or neighborhood, you know how those remarks can wound your heart. They can even make you feel sick. Often no one else is around to hear the cruel words, and there is no one to comfort.

Michelle was overweight, and people teased her and criticized her about it. "Oink! Oink!" the neighbor boy said when she walked by. "Blubber body!" the kids at school called her. "Michelle, you'll never slim down if you eat all that ice cream," her mom lectured her. "Don't you want to look pretty like your big sister?" Grandma asked her. An old nursery rhyme says, "Sticks and stones can break my bones, but words can never hurt me." Words may not make you bleed, but they definitely hurt—badly. In fact, wounds from abusive words can take far longer to heal than broken bones or cuts.

If insults have wounded you, go directly to Jesus with your hurt. He himself said he was sent to heal the broken-hearted. (See Luke 4:18; Isaiah 61:1.) Ask him to heal your heart from the pain caused by scornful words. Believe it or not, God can comfort you better than any person on earth. In fact, the Holy Spirit is called the "Comforter." Comforting is one of his most important jobs. "I will pray to the Father, and he shall give you another Comforter, that he may abide with you for ever" (John 14:16 KJV). God says you are worthy, valuable, and made in his image. And God loves you just the way you are!

Did You Know ...

verbal abuse comes in many forms, including name-calling, criticizing, threatening, and blaming? If you are dealing with this, seek a counselor or your pastor and tell them about it!

GirL TaLk:

Have you been hurt by abusive words in the past? How did they make you feel? In what ways do you still feel their impact?

More To Explore: Psalm 31:11, 14–15

God TaLk:

Lord, mean words can hurt so much. I give all my hurt feelings to you. Please heal me. Please help me to use only uplifting words toward others. Amen.

Devotion #58

"Hear me, my God, as I voice my complaint."
—Psalm 64:1 (TNIV)

TeLLing ALL

God loves us and cares very much how we feel—about everything! He hears us as we pour out our frustration, pain, and resentment. He knows our hearts and minds. Nothing we tell him can surprise him.

You know from many years of Sunday school that believers are supposed to "do everything without grumbling or arguing" (Philippians 2:14 TNIV). And yet, some days you feel so frustrated that you're ready to explode. Sometimes it's little things: your sister drinking all the orange juice or your best friend forgetting to return your favorite shirt. Sometimes it's big things: your mom yelling at you for no good reason or an unfair grade on a test. You bottle up your feelings, pretending things are great. When you pray, you feel like a phony.

You have a wrong idea about being honest with God. He's the one person to whom you can always tell the absolute truth. If it weren't all right to be totally honest with God, would David have written these psalms? "O Lord, hear me as I pray; pay attention to my groaning" (Psalm 5:1 NLT). "Give heed to me and answer me; I am restless in my complaint and am surely distracted" (Psalm 55:2 NASB). And in Psalm 142:2 (TNIV), David says, "I pour out before him my complaint; before him I tell my trouble." Being totally honest with God about your feelings is good. It isn't the same as grumbling about your life to everyone you meet. It's just sharing your feelings with him so you can sort them out together—and he can help you in each situation. Talk to God. He cares.

Did You Know ...

one of the best results of telling God everything that troubles you is that he can take away all your fear about the situation? (See Psalm 34:4.)

More To Explore: Psalm 130:1-2

Girl Talk:

When you pray, what do you talk to God about? Is it on-the-surface stuff, like "Help me pass my test tomorrow"? Or is it heartfelt, like "I'm so mad at Mom. Why can't she understand me?" How can you "go deeper" in your prayers?

God Talk:

Lord, I want to be able to talk to you about anything. Please help me remember that it's okay to share everything with you. Amen.

Devotion #59

"Children, obey your parents in everything,
for this pleases the Lord."
—Colossians 3:20 (TNIV)

Terrific Trade

Obedience to your parents isn't optional, according to God's Word. Children must obey their parents in everything. Obedience with a cheerful attitude and willing heart brings such pleasure to God. Hailey had been obedient as a small child, but when she was eleven, it suddenly became harder. She felt her mom was too picky about cleaning her room and limiting TV and phone time. Even though Hailey kept most of her irritation to herself, her stomach often hurt. When she finally decided to obey willingly instead, God was pleased. The upset stomach also disappeared.

Why would obeying parents please the Lord? For one thing, it's good training. If you're obedient to your parents when you're a child, it's easier as an adult believer to be obedient to God's Word and live a happy, abundant life. Even Jesus had to learn by experience what it meant to obey his father's will. "Although He was a Son, He learned obedience from the things which He suffered" (Hebrews

5:8 NASB). Being obedient—especially doing something we really don't want to do—will also bring us a form of suffering. It's unlikely that you'll ever suffer as much as Jesus did on the cross, but obedience will cost you some mental pain or emotional discomfort. The suffering usually results from not getting your own way about something. Be ready, stand firm, and you'll come through on the other side—victorious! The more you learn to respectfully obey, the easier it will become. Then the turmoil and conflict will be replaced with joy and peace—a terrific trade!

Did You Know ...

being obedient to your mother and father can actually keep you protected and safe, day and night? (See Proverbs 6:20–22.)

More To Explore: Exodus 20:12

Girl Talk:

What is one thing your parents ask you to do that you find really hard to obey? How can you approach it differently from now on? Feel that stress melt away!

God Talk:

Lord, some days it is so tough to do what Mom and Dad ask. Please give me the courage to obey willingly and with no complaint. I want to honor my parents and you. Thank you. Amen.

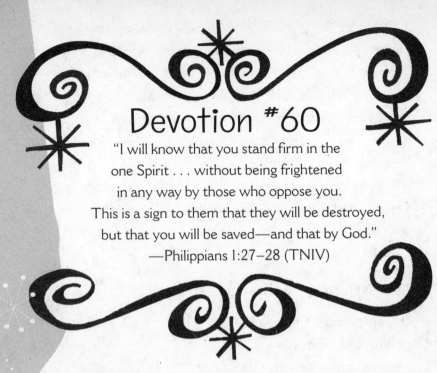

Devotion #60

"I will know that you stand firm in the
one Spirit . . . without being frightened
in any way by those who oppose you.
This is a sign to them that they will be destroyed,
but that you will be saved—and that by God."
—Philippians 1:27–28 (TNIV)

FearLess!

Don't be frightened or feel threatened by your enemies.
Your calm fearlessness will prove to them—it will be a
sign—that you will overcome. Your peaceful courage is evi-
dence that you are going to be saved, even by God himself.
You've been a believer since you were eight years old.
Because you were homeschooled, most of your friends are
from church or other homeschool families. When you
start middle school in fifth grade, you're shocked and
hurt by the kids who make fun of you. They
ridicule your longer skirts, your "What
Would Jesus Do?" bracelet, and the kit-
tens on your notebook cover. They call
you a baby—and worse. You grow to
fear going to school. When you finally
confide in your dad, he helps you find
the courage God has given you. From

then on, you face their comments with a calm assurance, knowing God will save you from the effects of their attacks. Your calm, unwavering attitude also has an effect you didn't expect. Your attackers grow uncomfortable, back down, and eventually quit. They even begin to treat you with respect.

"Listen to me, you who know right from wrong and cherish my law in your hearts. Do not be afraid of people's scorn or their slanderous talk" (Isaiah 51:7 NLT). This promise is given to those who follow God's laws and value his Word. If you're doing this—if you're following Jesus to the best of your ability—then you don't need to fear people's threats. Be calm and courageous!

Did You Know ...

acting calm and confident also works on athletic team opponents? It makes them think, *What does she know that we don't? She must be good!* Just don't forget that it's the Lord who is your confidence and security! (See Proverbs 3:26.)

More To Explore: Hebrews 13:6

Girl Talk:

How do others treat you? Are you afraid of anyone at school? What can you remind yourself of when others taunt or threaten you?

God Talk:

Lord, sometimes I'm scared of others and what they could do. Please give me your courage. I know you will take care of me. Amen.

Devotion #61

"This is the confidence we have in approaching God:
that if we ask anything according to his will, he hears us.
And if we know that he hears us—whatever we ask—
we know that we have what we asked of him."
—1 John 5:14–15 (TNIV)

Asking and Receiving

We can be sure that God will listen to us whenever we ask
him for anything in agreement with his own plan. Then,
since we positively know he is listening when we make our
requests, we can be sure that he'll give us what we ask for.

Gabby had always had a hot temper. She hated being told
what to do—by her parents, her teachers, her older brother,
her youth pastor. She didn't really mean to, but argumen-
tative words flew out of her mouth before she thought
about it. She was tired of the consequences of
shooting off her mouth: detention after
school, having her allowance taken away,
getting socked by her brother. Then she
read a verse in the Bible: "Everyone
should be quick to listen, slow to speak
and slow to become angry" (James 1:19

TNIV). Gabby correctly figured that if God wanted her to be slow to speak, God would give her the power.

How can we know what God's will is? We can find God's will in his Word. It's spelled out for us in his commands and needs to be "stored" in our minds and hearts. (We do this by reading and thinking about God's Word, plus memorizing it.) There is one more important step in seeing your prayers answered. You must have faith (or believe) that God answers prayer. "Without faith it is impossible to please God, because anyone who comes to him must believe that he exists and that he rewards those who earnestly seek him" (Hebrews 11:6 TNIV). Find out what God wants you to do—then be confident that he will help you do it!

Did You Know ...

in the Bible, Jesus is called the "divine Yes," because all of God's promises have been fulfilled in him? (See 2 Corinthians 1:19–20 NLT.)

More To Explore: Jeremiah 29:12–13

Girl Talk:

Are you reading the Bible regularly? What have you read recently that makes you think, *God's trying to tell me something?*

God Talk:

Lord, thank you for giving me the Bible. I can always look for true answers there and know how to pray according to your will. Amen.

Devotion #62

"The Lord looked with favor on Abel and his offering, but on Cain and his offering he did not look with favor. So Cain was very angry, and his face was downcast."
—Genesis 4:4–6 (TNIV)

Burning With Jealousy

Cain was a farmer, and his brother, Abel, kept flocks of animals. Both brothers brought offerings to God. Abel brought animals (which God required), but Cain brought things he had grown instead. When God accepted Abel's offering, but not Cain's, Cain was extremely jealous of his brother.

Maybe you know that jealous feeling. You feel guilty, but you can't stand your own little brother. He's been in and out of hospitals his whole life, and you know you should feel sympathy for him. Instead, you boil with jealous anger at all the attention he gets. Church members bring him gifts and candy. The neighbors loan him DVDs to watch. Mom and Dad hold him constantly. When they aren't actually with him, they talk about his condition all the time. *Hey, you have another kid!* you want to yell. *Remember me?*

Brothers and sisters often feel jealous of the attention a sibling receives. Even though it's perfectly natural, you must deal strongly with the jealousy. If you don't, it will be a cancer that eats away inside you. "He who hates his brother is in darkness and walks in darkness, and does not know where he is going, because the darkness has blinded his eyes" (1 John 2:11 NKJV). Instead of darkness, you need the light of God's love and forgiveness.

Confess the sin of jealousy to God. He will understand, and he will forgive. (See 1 John 1:9.) Then ask God to give you his love for your brother or sister. You can't love them on your own—not for very long anyway. Only with the help of the Holy Spirit can it be done. He wants to—and he will!

Did You Know ...

when the returning Prodigal Son was given a robe and food for a party for his friends, his older brother was jealous? Read Luke 15:26–32 to find out what happened.

More To Explore: Proverbs 27:4

Girl Talk:

Do you ever feel jealous about a brother or sister? How do you treat that sibling? Would God be proud of your behavior?

God Talk:

Lord, I know my family loves me, but sometimes it's hard to remember that I'm important to them too. Please take away my feelings of jealousy. I don't want to act or feel jealous anymore! Amen.

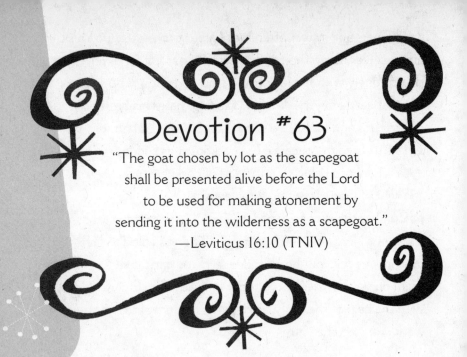

Devotion #63

"The goat chosen by lot as the scapegoat
shall be presented alive before the Lord
to be used for making atonement by
sending it into the wilderness as a scapegoat."
—Leviticus 16:10 (TNIV)

Scapegoat

In Old Testament times, the Day of Atonement came
once a year. It was the day to deal with the sins of the
whole year. One goat was killed in the tabernacle as a sin
offering to the Lord, and another goat (the scapegoat) was
sent away into the wilderness, carrying away the sins of the
people. The scapegoat was payment for their sins, a payment
that needed to be made every year.

Gabby knew about making payments. She wanted to
buy a mountain bike and had earned $25 toward it
so far. Mr. Brown, who owned the local bike
store, was saving the bike for her. This week
she would make her first small payment.
Sighing, she told her friend, "At this rate,
I'll never get to take the bike home!"

That Saturday when she went to make
her first payment, Mr. Brown wheeled

the bike out of storage and handed it over to her. Gabby was puzzled. "What's this? Even after my payment, I will still owe you $110." Mr. Brown showed her the sales ticket. In bright red ink, he'd written, PAID IN FULL. "Your parents came in and paid it off. They said they were proud of all your help around home." Gabby grinned and wheeled her new bike out of the store.

In the Old Testament, a person's sin debt had to be paid every year. But when Christ died on the cross, he wrote PAID IN FULL across your sins. "He canceled the record that contained the charges against us. He took it and destroyed it by nailing it to Christ's cross" (Colossians 2:14 NLT). Salvation is a free gift to us—but it cost Jesus his life. Thank him today for being your scapegoat—and carrying away your sins forever.

Did You Know ...

a goat was also used as a symbol in a dream of Daniel's? In Daniel 8, the goat represents Greece and the ruler Alexander the Great.

More To Explore: Isaiah 53:6

Girl Talk:

Do you have any debts? How would it feel to have someone pay them off?

God Talk:

Lord, thank you for being my scapegoat. I can't imagine how it felt, but I'm so grateful you died for me. Help me not to sin anymore. Amen.

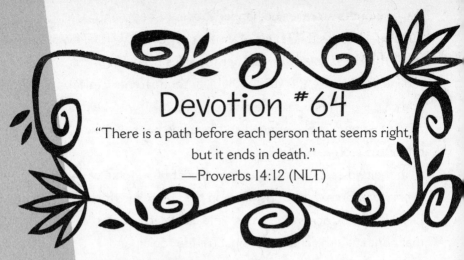

Devotion #64

"There is a path before each person that seems right,
but it ends in death."
—Proverbs 14:12 (NLT)

What Now?

Each person makes many choices every day.
Should I do this or that? Should I go here or there?
The path that seems right to us can end in disaster.
By ourselves, we just aren't smart enough to figure
things out!

You're thrilled when Kylie moves in next door. Kylie is
everything you're not. Where you're timid, Kylie's brave,
ready to try anything. Where you're shy, Kylie's outgoing. She
can speak to total strangers with ease. There's always something exciting happening with Kylie around. You feel lucky
that Kylie is your friend. Until . . . Kylie's "try anything"
attitude prompts her to shoplift some candy. When
caught, her "outgoing" personality causes her to
mouth off to the store owner. Both your parents are then called. Kylie seemed like such
a great friend, but the result of that
friendship is disaster.

So how can you know if you're on a
wrong path—when it appears okay?
First, check it out with God's Word.

There may be guidelines or a commandment concerning your situation. What about the times there isn't a specific Scripture to go by? (There are no verses telling which brand of running shoes to buy or which band instrument to play.) In those cases, find a trustworthy, godly person and ask for advice. Don't rely on your own understanding. Let God lead you.

Did You Know ...

the man called the wisest person who ever lived didn't always take the right path? God granted Solomon more wisdom than anyone else, but Solomon didn't always use his godly wisdom. He was still led astray by his many wives and their false gods and worldly thinking. (See Nehemiah 13:26.)

More To Explore: Proverbs 12:15

Girl Talk:

Can you think of two or three godly people you can turn to for advice? What qualities do they have? Keep them in mind when questions pop up.

God Talk:

Lord, I want to make sure I'm taking the right path. Please help me make the right choices and ask the right people. Amen.

Fun Factoid

The Bible says to call wisdom your sister, meaning you should hold wisdom in high regard. (See Proverbs 7:4.)

Devotion #65

"Stern discipline awaits those who leave the path;
those who hate correction will die."
—Proverbs 15:10 (TNIV)

Big Price To Pay!

There will be serious correction for the person who gives up living God's way. The person who hates to be disciplined or scolded for wrongdoing will die. It will be a physical death, a moral death, and a spiritual death.

Ella's parents were divorced when Ella was in fifth grade. Because Ella blamed God for not answering her prayer to keep the family together, she gave up living like a believer. She began to drink, hang out with older boys, sneak out at night, skip church, and skip school. At first, the discipline at home and school was moderate: detention, being grounded, a tighter curfew. When Ella rebelled and continued to do whatever she wanted, the discipline became more harsh. She was expelled from school and no one trusted her. Finally she was badly injured in a car accident in which the driver was drunk.

Sometimes we don't like to think of God as someone who disciplines us when we rebel and go our own way. "That's not loving!" some people declare.

Actually, the opposite is true. God disciplines us *because* he loves us, just as an earthly father corrects his kids to help them live a better life. If God didn't love us, he'd let us rebel and do nothing about it. But he knows that the consequences of living a life without him will kill us. The Lord will do what's necessary to convince you to get back on a path toward life. That's because he loves you so much.

Did You Know ...

Jonah almost died because he rebelled against God? Being swallowed by a great fish actually saved him from drowning. (See Jonah 1:17.) God gave him a second chance. He'll give you one too!

More To Explore: Proverbs 13:1

Girl Talk:

Has God had to discipline you in the past year? Did you get the message and turn back to him or is he still trying to get your attention?

God Talk:

Lord, I don't like being disciplined, but I know it's because you love me. Please help me listen to you and correct my ways. I want to follow you more closely. Amen.

Fun Factoid

Jonah was the first foreign missionary (going to a different country to witness about God).

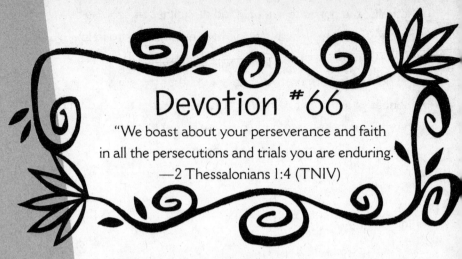

Devotion #66

"We boast about your perseverance and faith
in all the persecutions and trials you are enduring."
—2 Thessalonians 1:4 (TNIV)

The Tough Get Going

Even when severely tested, believers should be
faithful. Keep your trust in God firm. Continue
your course of action despite hardships you are living
through.

You've looked forward to middle school for two years.
In middle school you can be on a gymnastics team. You've
taken gymnastics classes since you were four years old, and
you secretly dream of competing in the Olympics one day.
But from the first day of practice, you're so disappointed. The
coach doesn't like you for some reason. He criticizes you
constantly, even though you know you're better than anyone else who tried out. A few weeks into practice, you
see the coach give one of the girls a big hug, and
you ask a team member about it. "You mean
Rachel? That's Coach's kid. He's determined that she's going to be a gold medal
winner or something." Now you understand the persecution you've been
receiving. Coach wants his own daugh-
ter to be the best. You pray about it, and

you decide to stay on the team. You'll just dig in and work hard, keeping your eye on your long-term Olympic goal.

There's an old saying: "When the going gets tough, the tough get going." That means persevering through trials and mistreatment. (Note: persecution means the trials you endure that are not your fault. Punishment for wrongdoing is not persecution—it's just consequences for wrong actions.) "We can rejoice, too, when we run into problems and trials, for we know that they are good for us—they help us learn to endure. And endurance develops strength of character in us" (Romans 5:3–4 NLT). So be tough— and get going!

Did You Know . . .

it helps during times of trouble to think beyond your pain to the outcome? "We don't look at the troubles we can see right now . . . For the troubles we see will soon be over, but the joys to come will last forever" (2 Corinthians 4:18 NLT).

More To Explore: James 5:11

Girl Talk:

Have you ever been severely tested? How did you react to the tough situation? What can you change about your attitude for the next time a trial comes along?

God Talk:

Lord, I want to stay close to you, no matter what is happening in my life. Help me keep a good attitude throughout any trial I encounter. Thank you for your unending support. Amen.

Devotion #67

"Be kind and compassionate to one another,
forgiving each other, just as in Christ God forgave you.
—Ephesians 4:32 (TNIV)

Sharing The Love

If you're a believer, God has forgiven all your
sins—past, present, and future. He's so kind to
you, so caring about every detail of your life. Treat
others in this same way. Show God's love, kindness, and
forgiveness to everyone you meet.

Kayla's Sunday school teacher said, "Your life may be the
only Bible your friends read. Are they learning anything about
God by watching you?" Kayla knew she didn't do any really bad
stuff—no drinking, no drugs, no smoking, no swearing. But did
her unbelieving friends (none of whom went to church) learn
anything about God's love by being around her? From that
day on, Kayla determined that her life and her actions
would demonstrate God to her friends. She made a
list of things she could do to show God's love,
forgiveness, and compassion in some form
each day to a friend. Sometimes she gave
a compliment or a word of encouragement. Sometimes she helped a friend
carry something or gave a hand with
homework. Sometimes it was forgiving a
friend instead of being mad.

If your friends never read the Bible, would they still learn through your actions that "love is patient, love is kind" (1 Corinthians 13:4 TNIV)? Give to others what God has so freely given to you. He's devoted to your well-being, he forgives instead of getting revenge, he's sympathetic to your problems, he's patient, and he's kind. Let God have control of your life so you can love others the way he loves you!

Did You Know ...

in *Sophie Flakes Out* the Corn Flakes added another rule to their secret Code? "Corn Flakes are totally loyal to each other and will always empathize."

Girl Talk:

Think about your circle of friends. To whom can you reach out and show God's love? Write down a few things to try this coming week.

More To Explore: Romans 12:10

God Talk:

Lord, please help me to show my friends your love. Thank you for your love and forgiveness to me and everyone. Amen.

Mini-Quiz:

Who best showed God's love to another?

a. Samson
b. the good Samaritan
c. Roman soldiers

Answer: b. the good Samaritan

Devotion #68

"Moses and Aaron went to Pharaoh and said to him,
'This is what the Lord, the God of the Hebrews, says:
"How long will you refuse to humble yourself before me?
Let my people go, so that they may worship me.
If you refuse to let them go, I will bring
locusts into your country tomorrow."'"
—Exodus 10:3–4 (TNIV)

Here Come The Plagues!

God gave Pharaoh plenty of warning. He told the king to let his people go free so they could worship him. God said if Pharaoh refused, he would cover the whole country with locusts that would eat everything.

You've received a few warnings yourself—from your dad. "Limit your phone calls to ten minutes," he says, "and then finish your homework." You lose track of time, and an hour slips by. Dad warns you again about losing phone privileges, but you keep talking. Finally, Dad unplugs your phone and takes it away with him. You had several chances to obey the phone rule. When you refused, consequences forced you to obey.

God did the same thing with the king. "Then the Lord said to Moses, 'Pharaoh is very stubborn, and he continues to refuse to let the people go'" (Exodus 7:14 NLT). God gave Pharaoh many, many chances. In total, God unleashed ten crushing plagues against Egypt before Pharaoh finally obeyed. Don't be stubborn like Pharaoh! Instead, be obedient to those in charge of you: parents, teachers, and pastors. It's much easier to humble yourself than to have God humble you!

Did You Know ...

God brought plagues on the Israelites as well? When the Israelites disobeyed him, God often sent a plague to show them clearly that they had disobeyed. (See Exodus 32:35; and Numbers 11:33; 16:46.)

More To Explore: Exodus 10:12–15

Girl Talk:

Have you ever lost privileges or suffered consequences because you ignored warnings? Is it easier to obey or to suffer later? Ask God to help you obey the first time.

God Talk:

Lord, I don't always obey the first time someone asks me, and I want to change that. Please help me obey without attitude. I want to make you and those in charge of me proud. Thank you. Amen.

Fun Factoid

A swarm of locusts may number more than one hundred thousand insects per square mile and can eat thousands of acres of vegetation in a single day! Now that's a plague!

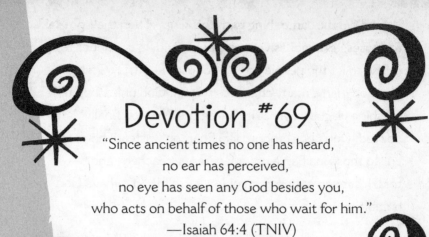

Devotion #69

"Since ancient times no one has heard,
no ear has perceived,
no eye has seen any God besides you,
who acts on behalf of those who wait for him."
—Isaiah 64:4 (TNIV)

Worth Waiting For

There's no god like our God! For since the world began, no one has ever heard of (and no one has ever seen) a God like ours, who works for those who wait for him!

Stephanie's parents had separated, but not yet divorced. They were trying to work out their problems, but Stephanie feared that things were going from bad to worse. She helped out at home with her little sister and cleaning the apartment, and she prayed every night for her parents to be reunited. The eleven months she waited— praying every night and expecting God to work a miracle—were the longest months of her life. At times, she didn't think God had even heard her. Yet she continued to look forward to her family being restored. At the end of eleven long months, when her parents were back together, did Stephanie think that waiting on God had been worth it? You bet! "The Lord is good to those whose hope is in him, to the one who seeks him" (Lamentations 3:25 TNIV).

In *Webster's* dictionary, *waiting* is defined as "remaining inactive in one place while expecting something and looking forward to something." Believers are waiting and expecting God to go to work for them, to work things out and make things happen that only God can make happen. "The Lord longs to be gracious to you . . . Blessed are all who wait for him!" (Isaiah 30:18 TNIV). Whatever you're facing, pray and wait for God to act. He won't let you down.

Did You Know . . .

Noah had to wait a year to get out of the ark? (Compare Genesis 7:11 and 8:14.) Noah and his family were inside for a year and ten days total before God said to come out of the ark. That's waiting!

More To Explore: Isaiah 40:31

Girl Talk:

When was the last time you waited for God to do something? Did you wait for it to happen or did you try to "help" because it seemed to take too long?

God Talk:

Lord, I know your timing is perfect. Sometimes it's really hard for me to wait. Please give me patience as I wait for you. Thank you for staying with me. Amen.

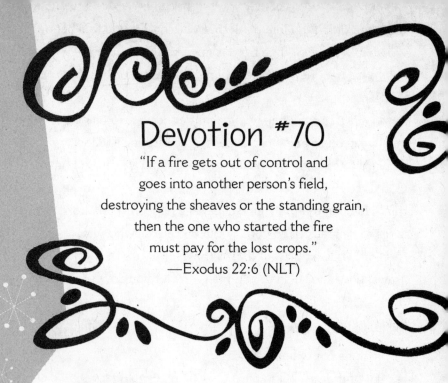

Devotion #70

"If a fire gets out of control and
goes into another person's field,
destroying the sheaves or the standing grain,
then the one who started the fire
must pay for the lost crops."
—Exodus 22:6 (NLT)

Pay Back

Laws were created to make sure that people were treated
fairly. Certain laws in the Old Testament pointed out that if
you were at fault (if your actions caused the problem), you
needed to pay the person back for what was destroyed.
Empty apologies were not enough.

Maybe you borrow your sister's new sweater (with per-
mission) to wear to a birthday party for your best friend.
While carrying food out to the tables by the pool,
you catch your heel on an uneven brick and fall
hard—right on top of the chocolate cake.
No matter how you scrub, the stain
won't come out of the sweater. You're
really sorry, and you apologize when
you get home. However, when your sister suggests that you replace the sweater

or pay to have it cleaned, you bristle. You don't think that's necessary. You feel that an apology should fix the problem.

Talk is cheap. Apologies—when heartfelt—are wonderful and necessary. But when you've destroyed someone else's property, apologies aren't enough. You need to pay for the damages and restore the property. The next day when your little brother borrows your new markers and loses them on the way home from school, you demand that he buy you some new markers. Then, thinking back, you also agree sheepishly to make up for staining the new sweater. You can't afford to buy a new sweater for your sister, but you can pay the dry-cleaning bill.

Put yourself in the other person's shoes. If someone ruined or lost something that belonged to you, wouldn't you like to have the item replaced? It's fair!

Did You Know ...

our country is now trying to make up for the sins of slavery? Slavery ended in 1865, but 140 years later, restitution (payment for a loss) is now being discussed.

More To Explore: Exodus 21:33–36

Girl Talk:

Think of the last time you apologized for something. Looking back, was the apology enough or do you need to go further?

God Talk:

Lord, I know I don't always act fairly toward others. Please help me remember how fair you are to everyone, including me. I want to do better. Amen.

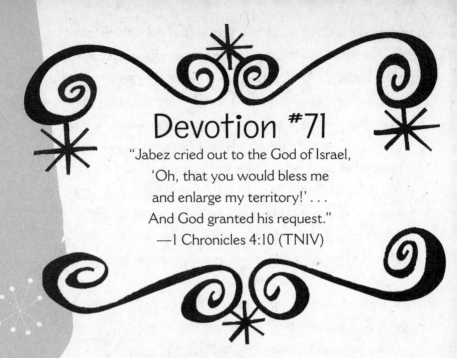

Devotion #71

"Jabez cried out to the God of Israel,
'Oh, that you would bless me
and enlarge my territory!' . . .
And God granted his request."
—1 Chronicles 4:10 (TNIV)

The Price of Blessing

We all want to be blessed. Jabez was no different. One thing he asked God for was "enlarged territory." That can mean more land, but it can also mean having more power or a more important job.

Rachel wanted the most important role in the musical her middle school planned to perform. She wanted to play the lead singer, Maria, in *The Sound of Music*. She worked hard before tryouts, learning lines and music. When the auditions were over, she nearly fainted with joy when her name was listed beside "Maria Von Trapp."

Soon, however, Rachel realized the honor came with many added responsibilities. She worked longer hours. She attended individual rehearsals with the vocal and drama teachers. After practicing many nights till nine o'clock, she still had all her homework to do. When God answers a prayer for more blessings, people are thrilled! (At least for a while.) Soon they realize that blessings also carry new responsibilities. So don't pray for the blessing if you're not ready for the added responsibility.

So where's my blessing? you might ask. Could it be that God is waiting on you, and "you do not have because you do not ask God" (James 4:2 TNIV)? Before you ask, do a heart checkup. Is there any sin you need to confess? "If I had cherished sin in my heart, the Lord would not have listened; but God has surely listened and has heard my prayer" (Psalm 66:18–19 TNIV). God loves to bless his children. It gives him great joy—so go ahead and ask!

Did You Know ...

although the prayer of Jabez (see 1 Chronicles 4:10) is famous in our time, it was a sermon topic 130 years ago? The famous preacher Charles Spurgeon said that you could expect a blessing in serving God if you could persevere through discouragements. Trials are part of the blessing package!

Girl Talk:

What do you want to be blessed with? Have you confessed all lingering sin, so that God is free to work?

More To Explore: Matthew 7:7–11

God Talk:

Lord, I thank you for all the good things you have already given me. Please bless me now with ____. Thank you for your continued loving presence. Amen.

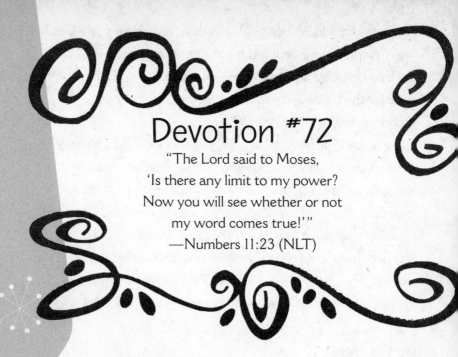

Devotion #72

"The Lord said to Moses,
'Is there any limit to my power?
Now you will see whether or not
my word comes true!'"
—Numbers 11:23 (NLT)

ALL Powerful

The Israelites complained to Moses about the manna
God provided for them to eat each day. They were tired of
it and wanted meat, so God said he would send meat. Moses
doubted that God could find enough meat to feed several million hungry people. God's response? "Stand back and watch
my word come true. My power is unlimited."

You might need the unlimited power of God in your own
life. Your dad has been arrested for stealing money from
his company, but he vows that he's innocent. You and
your mom believe him. However, his computer
at work shows that he transferred company
money to his own private bank account. It
looks as if he will go to jail. Still, you
believe God's promise: "The Lord will
vindicate his people and have compassion on his servants" (Psalm 135:14

NLT). You know your dad loves Jesus. You believe God will defend your dad and prove he's innocent. Just before the trial begins, a computer whiz detects an odd pathway in the transaction; he proves someone else had hacked into the computer and stolen the money. Your dad's set free. Your whole family praises God for his awesome power.

When circumstances look impossible, it's a great opportunity for God to show his strength. God made promises to his people, and he keeps his word. "God is not a man, that he should lie. He is not a human, that he should change his mind. Has he ever spoken and failed to act? Has he ever promised and not carried it through?" (Numbers 23:19 NLT). So lean on the Lord. Nothing is too hard for him!

Did You Know . . .

God answered the Israelites' complaint with quail? A wind blew the quail in from the sea, and the birds rained down around the camp. The quail were piled three feet deep all around! (See Numbers 11:31.)

More To Explore: Genesis 18:14; Joshua 21:45

Girl Talk:

What things in your life look impossible to you right now? Have you asked God to show you his power? How do you think that might help?

God Talk:

Lord, help me remember that you always keep your promises. Please be with me through everything today. Thank you for your love and power. Amen.

Devotion #73

"The Lord is gracious and compassionate,
slow to anger and rich in love."
—Psalm 145:8 (TNIV)

True Riches

The Lord is kind and generous and caring. He has
deep sympathy for our suffering. Always patient,
he is slow to get angry with us. He is filled with
kindness and love.

Hannah felt like a failure and needed God's understanding. She was a quitter, and she hated that quality in herself.
She set big goals and worked hard at them—until things got
hard. For her social studies project on Texas, she planned to
build an oil well that showed actual drilling. Halfway through,
she got discouraged and quit, settling for a C instead of an A.
She went out for the junior track team, but four days into
practice she had blisters, and her legs hurt so badly she
quit. And now she'd done it again, even though she'd
tried really hard to stick it out. She'd started a
paper route, but hated getting up at 5:00
a.m. every day to do her route before
school. Within a week, she quit. She felt
guilty, and she wanted to talk to God
about it, but she was afraid. Surely God
was mad at her for dropping out again.
He probably didn't want to talk to her.

Hannah didn't know the Lord as well as she thought. He wasn't shaking his finger at her in anger. She wasn't "out of chances." God isn't like that. Instead, the Lord picks us up, dusts us off, and gives us encouragement to try again. "The Lord is merciful and gracious; he is slow to get angry and full of unfailing love" (Psalm 103:8 NLT). Don't be afraid to go to your heavenly Father with your failures. He loves you. He'll help you start over as many times as it takes.

Did You Know ...

Thomas Edison was a great example of a person who didn't let failure or mistakes get him down? He once said, "If I find ten thousand ways that something won't work, I haven't failed . . . every wrong attempt discarded is a step forward."

More To Explore: Psalm 86:5

Girl Talk:

When you set out to do something, how successful are you? How hard do you work?

God Talk:

Lord, I don't want to be a quitter. Please be with me as I work. I want to work hard and make you proud. Amen.

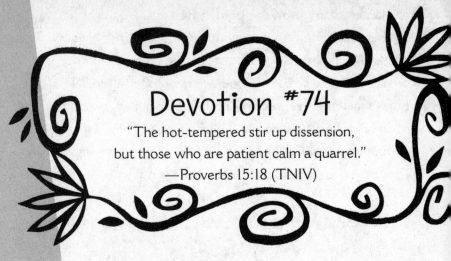

Devotion #74

"The hot-tempered stir up dissension,
but those who are patient calm a quarrel."
—Proverbs 15:18 (TNIV)

PUTTING OUT FIRES

A hothead—someone who gets angry easily—
starts fights. A cool-tempered person tries to stop
arguments. A patient person will try to calm people
down—not stir things up.

Maybe your dad likes to pick fights. He fights with your
mom, your older brother, his boss, and the neighbors. When
he's drinking, it's even worse. You try to do everything he
wants, but sometimes nothing is good enough. Things can be
calm and peaceful one minute, and then within ten minutes of
his arriving home, he's shouting and fighting with someone.

The only person able to calm him down is Uncle Mark. He
stops by frequently, patiently listens to your dad, and
helps him get things fixed around the house. You
wish Uncle Mark could live with your family
full-time.

It's very difficult to live with people
who are quick-tempered. They seem to
be looking for a fight—and they usually
find one. As far as it depends on you,
however, be a person who stops quarrels.

Don't add fuel to the fire—instead, help put it out. The "fire" might be at home with a brother, at school with a best friend, or with someone on your soccer team. "Be quick to listen, slow to speak, and slow to get angry. Your anger can never make things right in God's sight" (James 1:19–20 NLT). Make it your goal this week to be a calming influence on an angry person. Be a peacemaker!

Did You Know ...

in order to be a calming influence on an angry person, you have to be calm as well? (See James 3:18.) Before you try to help, decide to not judge the other person or what they are saying.

More To Explore: Matthew 5:9

Girl Talk:

Can you think of a person close to you who loses his or her temper easily? In what ways might you help calm this person down?

God Talk:

Lord, I want to be a calming influence on those around me. Please help me keep control of my own emotions. Amen.

Fun Factoid

Use the acronym CALM to help calm someone down:

C: Calm yourself first.
A: Acknowledge what the other person is saying.
L: Listen actively—don't interrupt.
M: Make sure you understand.

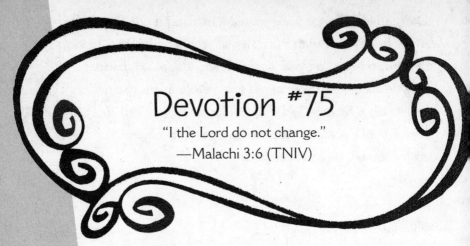

Devotion #75

"I the Lord do not change."
—Malachi 3:6 (TNIV)

No Variation

You can always count on the Lord to stay the same. He isn't a human being, whose moods shift and behavior alters from one day to the next. God's nature never changes, no matter what you do. You'll have many ups and downs in your life—but God remains steady and constant.

Mia and Lori were best friends all through grade school, and Mia assumed they always would be. But when they started going to a middle school that blended four elementary schools, things changed. Lori wanted to include new girls in everything they did. Then Mia found out that Lori was going to movies and shopping with them—but not inviting her along. Most times when Mia invited Lori to spend the night, Lori referred vaguely to "other plans." Plans that no longer included Mia . It was hard for Mia to admit that things had changed with Lori, and changed drastically. Accepting the change was painful.

People do change, and sometimes people will let us down. They're human, not perfect. No matter how many people change, remember that God is always constant. No matter where you live, no matter what you're going through—God never changes. You can bet your life on it, and you can settle down and rest. In a world that sometimes seems in constant change and upheaval, it's vital to remember that our God stays the same. "Jesus Christ is the same yesterday and today and forever" (Hebrews 13:8 TNIV). If you're a believer—if you're a follower of Jesus—your inner life can also be stable and solid and unchanging. No matter what.

Did You Know ...

eternity goes on forever and ever? (See Psalm 102:27.)

More To Explore: James 1:17

Girl Talk:

What has changed for you in the last few months? Was it a welcome change, or are you still adjusting? Have you asked God to help you through it?

God Talk:

Lord, just when I think I have my life under control, something changes. Please help me to go with the flow and rely on you and your unchanging love and security. Amen.

Devotion #76

"[There is] one Lord, one faith, one baptism."
—Ephesians 4:5 (AMP)

I Am THE Way

Society today teaches that there are many ways to God. It is popular to believe that all religions are basically alike and that "all roads lead to God." Not true! There is only one Lord (Jesus). The only faith that will save you is faith in the death and resurrection of Jesus Christ.

Maybe you've gone to church and Sunday school all your life. Then you go to middle school. Your literature teacher talks about "the Man upstairs," and your drama coach talks about a Higher Power. Both teacher and coach feel there are many spiritual paths a person might take to find a relationship with God. The coach explains that it is like a wagon wheel. God is the center of the wheel, and the spokes are different religions. She says people can travel any "spoke" (or path) they want to, and eventually they'll all be with God forever. While that kind of talk sounds soothing to many, it's 100 percent false.

There is only one way to God. "Jesus said . . . 'I am the way, the truth, and the life. No one comes to the Father except through Me'" (John 14:6 NKJV). No one? Not a single person? That's pretty strong—and very clear-cut. Then how do people get fooled into thinking they can create their own path to God? Satan comes with confusion and lies. "I am afraid that just as Eve was deceived by the serpent's cunning, your minds may somehow be led astray from your sincere and pure devotion to Christ" (2 Corinthians 11:3 TNIV). Don't be fooled by the devil or led away from God. Trust in God's Word to guide you into all truth. Jesus is the Way—and the only way!

Did You Know ...

according to *World Christian Encyclopedia*, there are nineteen major world religions? Christianity is the only one that talks about developing a personal relationship with God through Jesus Christ. The others focus on rules to keep to be right with God.

Girl Talk:

Has anyone ever tried to convince you that there are many ways to get to heaven? How did you respond to them? Ask God for the words to say.

More To Explore: Philippians 2:5–11; Acts 4:12

God Talk:

Lord, when people try to tell me false things about you, I want to be ready. Please give me the right words to tell them about the true way: Jesus. Thank you. Amen.

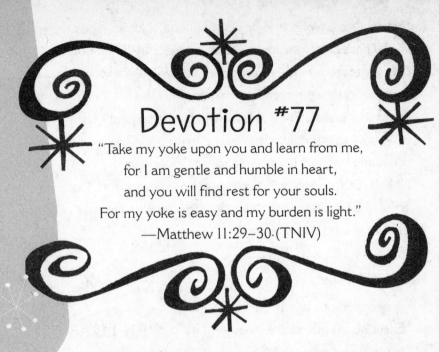

Devotion #77

"Take my yoke upon you and learn from me,
for I am gentle and humble in heart,
and you will find rest for your souls.
For my yoke is easy and my burden is light."
—Matthew 11:29–30 (TNIV)

Yoked With Jesus

A yoke is a connection between two things so they move together. Oxen and horses are often yoked so they can pull a heavy load together. Jesus wants you to take his yoke—to be connected to him so you can move in sync with him. His yoke—his connection to you—is light and easy to carry. His yoke is good—not hard, harsh, sharp, or heavy. If you're yoked with Jesus, you will find rest, relief, and refreshment for your mind and emotions.

What exactly does "putting on Jesus' yoke" look like? It means being obedient to his words. "If you keep My commandments, you will abide in My love, just as I have kept My Father's commandments and abide in His love. These things I have spoken to you, that My joy may remain in you, and that your joy may be full" (John 15:10–11

NKJV). Keeping his commands brings joy, but sometimes we think, *It's too hard to keep God's commandments. I just can't do it!* You're right—you can't do it, at least not by yourself. The Holy Spirit will help you, though, and give you the strength to do what's right. When you stop struggling in the yoke, forward movement can be easy! "This is love for God: to keep his commands. And his commands are not burdensome" (1 John 5:3 TNIV). Settle Jesus' yoke on your own shoulders—and experience a deep, refreshing rest.

Did You Know ...

Paul wrote that Christ has set us free from the "yoke of slavery"? The yoke he talked of in Galatians 5:1 included all the man-made laws Jews were required to keep at the time, which were an unbearable burden.

More To Explore: Philippians 4:13

Girl Talk:

In what ways lately have you and Jesus been pulling together? In what areas are you struggling alone? Ask for the Holy Spirit's help and strength, and you can snuggle instead of struggle!

God Talk:

Lord, I know that I sometimes struggle against you. Please give me the help and strength I need so that we can pull in the yoke together. Thank you for being on my team. Amen.

Devotion #78

"Don't have anything to do with foolish
and stupid arguments, because you know
they produce quarrels. And the Lord's servant
must not be quarrelsome but must be kind
to everyone, able to teach, not resentful."
—2 Timothy 2:23–24 (TNIV)

Fools Fight

Followers of Jesus should not get involved in foolish, igno-
rant arguments that only start fights. Christians must not
quarrel but must show everybody kindness. They must be
able to teach well while being patient with difficult people.
You never start quarrels and arguments, and you never
mean to get caught up in them. You love Jesus, and you
want to be a good witness for him at school. But
when people say the Bible is just another book,
or that Jesus never really lived, you get
upset. You defend yourself, and you try to
defend the Bible. Flustered, you turn
bright red. By the end of a conversation,
you can barely keep from telling your
friends that they're doomed.

The next time someone tries to argue with you about your faith, what should you do? "Live wisely among those who are not Christians, and make the most of every opportunity. Let your conversation be gracious and effective so that you will have the right answer for everyone" (Colossians 4:5–6 NLT). Continue to share your faith—but avoid foolish arguments about it.

Did You Know ...

when you "witness" to others, you are reporting the good news that Jesus rose from the dead? Before going to heaven, Jesus told the disciples to be his witnesses to all the world. (See Acts 1:8.)

More To Explore: James 3:17

GirL TaLk:

Has anyone ever questioned your beliefs? How did you respond? Ask God, before you discuss, to give you the right words.

God TaLk:

Lord, I want to speak loving truth about you. Please give me the right words to say or let me know if I need to stay quiet. Amen.

Mini-QuiZ:

1. Which billboard sign is a better witness?
   a. The end is at hand! Repent or die!
   b. Jesus rose from the grave! Believe and live!

2. Your friend is of a different faith. Which should you say to start a conversation?
   a. "Please tell me more about your faith. Which should you believe it's true?"
   b. "I can't understand why you believe such ridiculous stuff!"

Answers: 1. b; 2. a

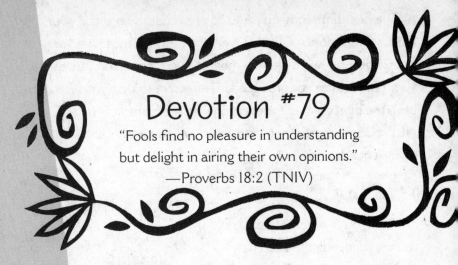

Devotion #79

"Fools find no pleasure in understanding
but delight in airing their own opinions."
—Proverbs 18:2 (TNIV)

Hot Air

Some people (the Bible calls them fools) would
rather give their own views to anyone who will listen than understand the truth. The fool's happiness is
in listening to her own voice—not in understanding a
matter. Often there is no truth to her opinions—just
guesses and rumors—and when the truth comes out, she
appears foolish.

Destiny met such a person when she befriended the new
girl, Peni, who came to church. Destiny invited her to their
youth group and over to her house to meet her friends from
school. It wasn't long before Destiny regretted knowing
Peni. No matter what the group did, Peni dominated.
She had strong opinions about everything, which
she voiced loudly as if hers were the only
opinions. Half the time she didn't know
what she was talking about. If Destiny
questioned anything Peni said, Peni
invented "facts" to support her opinions. She only ended up looking more
foolish—and causing people to avoid her.

No one cares to be around a windbag who never lets up. Destiny talked to Peni, explaining kindly how her behavior was driving people away. Peni got angry, stormed off, and found another group of girls to air her opinions to. "The fear of the Lord is the beginning of knowledge, but fools despise wisdom and instruction" (Proverbs 1:7 TNIV).

Don't be a girl who just talks to hear herself talk. Find out the truth and understand a situation before giving an opinion. And if you don't understand a situation, silence is always golden!

Did You Know ...

in *Sophie Tracks a Thief*, Sophie was injured at the school festival? All kinds of untrue rumors were spread by kids who didn't understand the situation—and who then looked foolish.

More To Explore: Ecclesiastes 10:3

Girl Talk:

Do you have pushy opinions about everything? Do you know someone who does? How do you deal with that person?

God Talk:

Lord, I like having my opinions matter, but help me remember that listening is even more important. Amen.

Fun Factoid

According to researchers, the average person can think four times faster than she can talk. This means that it's easy to stop listening, because you believe you already know what the other person is saying or going to say. Real listening takes a lot of work!

Devotion #80

"I tell you, her many sins have been forgiven—
as her great love has shown.
But whoever has been forgiven little loves little."
—Luke 7:47 (TNIV)

Thank You!

A woman came to see Jesus and fell down before him. With tears of thankfulness and gratitude, she washed his dusty feet with her tears, wiped them dry with her hair, and soothed them with fragrant oil. Her sins had been forgiven, and she was so thankful. The woman wanted to show her love for Jesus, and she chose to do it by washing his feet.

Brooke needed forgiveness too after hurriedly setting the table for Thanksgiving dinner. Tons of relatives always met at Grandma's house to eat, and she didn't mind helping, but she wanted to see the Thanksgiving Day parade on TV. Without thinking, she banged the flowered glass bowl down too hard on the ceramic counter, and the bowl cracked down the middle. When Brooke picked it up, it broke apart. The bowl belonged to her grandmother, and it had been in the family for generations. What would her grandmother say? Brooke wanted to cry. If only she'd been more careful! When Grandma stepped into the kitchen, Brooke told her about the bowl. Grandma gave Brooke a hug and said she knew it wasn't done on purpose. "I love you more than any old bowl," she said. Not another word was said about it. Brooke loved her grandmother even more after being forgiven.

What has God forgiven you for lately? A drop of praise isn't nearly enough for the ocean of mercy and love God has shown us. How can you show your appreciation to God today? Can you give a special offering? Can you help someone in need? Remember God's forgiveness today—and thank him for it.

Did You Know ...

the word *thank* (including *thankful* and *thankfulness*) is mentioned forty times in the Bible? (See, for example, Daniel 2:23; Psalm 100:4; and Colossians 3:15.)

Girl Talk:

What can you do today to show God how thankful you are?

More To Explore: Luke 7:41-43

God Talk:

Lord, thank you again and again for your forgiveness. I don't deserve it, but I appreciate it so much! Thank you for loving me that much.
Amen.

Beauty 101

A thankful heart and lips that praise can make anyone—young or old—beautiful. Think of one specific sin you once committed. Then stand in front of a mirror and tell God how thankful you are for his forgiveness. Watch your face light up! Beautiful!

Devotion #81

"A scoffer seeks Wisdom in vain
[for his very attitude blinds and deafens him to it],
but knowledge is easy to him who
[being teachable] understands."
—Proverbs 14:6 (AMP)

Are You Teachable?

A mocker is one who sneers with disrespect at something. Her superior attitude blinds her to wisdom because she refuses to fear the Lord or accept any correction. You can't be arrogant and grow in wisdom. On the other hand, someone who is teachable—humble and willing to learn—will find it easy to gain knowledge.

Savannah was knitting a scarf for her mom's birthday. Savannah's grandma had taught her how to knit and helped her choose the colors. When changing colors in the stripes, Savannah had trouble. It was lumpy where she tied off one color and began another. At first, when her grandmother offered some help, Savannah said she could handle it! But an hour later, after unraveling rows of stitches, Savannah went to find Grandma. "I need some help," she said sheepishly. "Can you show me how to do it right?" Savannah watched closely as Grandma demonstrated. With a bit of practice, her stitches looked almost as smooth as Grandma's.

Often scoffers believe they really are wise. They've figured out cunning ways to get what they want in the world. "Do not deceive yourselves. If any of you think you are wise by the standards of this age, you should become 'fools' so that you may become wise. For the wisdom of this world is foolishness in God's sight" (1 Corinthians 3:18–19 TNIV). So how do you get God's wisdom? Ask him for it. And ask often. He won't mind if you come to him for advice—in fact, he's eager to give you help. So be smart. Be teachable!

Did You Know ...

"He who dies with the most toys, wins" is a popular phrase among those "of the world"? This world's "wisdom" is often a load of foolishness!

More To Explore: Proverbs 26:12

Girl Talk:

Think of the last time you learned to do something. Were you teachable? In what ways? Did you rely on yourself? In what ways?

God Talk:

Lord, I don't always ask for help when I need it. Please help me realize that asking for help shows more wisdom than blundering through on my own. Thank you for your help every day. Amen.

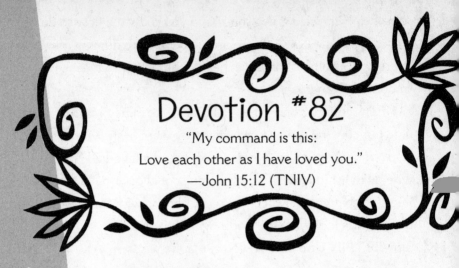

Devotion #82

"My command is this:
Love each other as I have loved you."
—John 15:12 (TNIV)

Love One Another

Jesus taught his followers to imitate him in how they treated others. He commanded (or required) them to love one another in the same way that he had loved them. That's a tall order!

You try to love your family and friends, but some are easier than others. Your baby sister always smiles—easy to love. Your older brother picks on you—hard to love. Your teacher encourages you—easy to love. Your dad rarely notices you unless you make a mistake—hard to love. But you know from Sunday school that Jesus loved a lot of hard-to-love people too, and he wants you to do the same.

It's wonderful to love others when we have warm feelings for them. However, we won't feel that way about everyone. We can love them God's way just the same. It's not about feelings. First, we can show respect to others. "Honor one another above yourselves" (Romans 12:10 TNIV). Second, we can serve others. We can set aside our selfish desires and serve others by sharing our time, kind words, and what we have. "Most important of all, continue to show deep love for each other, for love covers a multitude of sins. Cheerfully share your home with those who need a meal or a place to stay. God has given gifts to each of you from his great variety of spiritual gifts. Manage them well so that God's generosity can flow through you" (1 Peter 4:8–10 NLT). It's easy to show love to the people in your life who make you feel good. But you can follow Jesus' command with everyone by being respectful and sharing your gifts with them.

Did You Know ...

1 Corinthians 13 (the Love Chapter) isn't really about romantic love? It's about showing godly love to everyone. It says that love is not easily angered and that love doesn't keep track of wrongs. Remember that description when dealing with those who are hard to love.

More To Explore: Ephesians 5:1–2

Girl Talk:

Think of two or three people you find hard to love. What can you do to reach out to them?

God Talk:

Lord, it's not easy to love all people. Please help me find ways to show respect and caring to everyone around me. Amen.

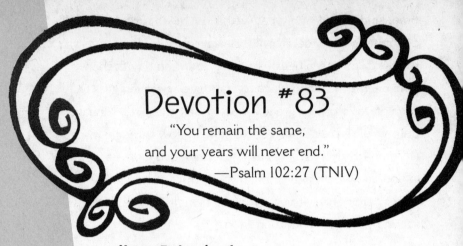

Devotion #83

"You remain the same,
and your years will never end."
—Psalm 102:27 (TNIV)

Never-Ending Lord

God is always the same. He was a loving God from the beginning. He's a loving God now. He will be a loving God forever. His years will never come to an end.

Jennifer had seen too many things come to an end in the past year. She wished she could have even two months in a row without changes. Her mom had left the family to pursue an acting career in California. Soon after the divorce, her dad remarried a woman with two little kids. They moved to a bigger home in another part of town, so Jennifer changed schools. She had to babysit after school now instead of being in soccer. They'd stopped going to church, and Jennifer missed her youth group even more than she'd expected. Sometimes Jennifer felt like the victim of a war. Her former life had been wiped out. Would anything ever be the same again?

There is one thing that never changes—and that's God. In a world that is sometimes overwhelming with its changes, it's important to remember that

Jesus is always the same. He's the Rock that never moves. Part of building on a rock includes being with other believers—you need their support—and Jennifer needs to find another church soon. Anyone who lives by Jesus' words is "like a man building a house, who dug deep and laid the foundation on the rock. And when the flood arose, the stream beat vehemently against that house, and could not shake it, for it was founded on the rock" (Luke 6:48 NKJV). Sometimes changes come so rapidly that it feels like a flood. But if you build your life on the Rock, you won't come apart! You'll weather the storm and still be standing!

Did You Know ...

Jesus says he was here before us and will be here after us? "Do not be afraid; I am the First and the Last. I *am* He who lives, and was dead, and behold, I am alive forevermore" (Revelation 1:17–18 NKJV).

More To Explore: Psalm 18:2

Girl Talk:

Have you ever felt flooded by changes? Who did you turn to? Did you know that God will always be your shelter in that flood?

God Talk:

Lord, sometimes I feel knocked over by all these changes in my life—my body, my friends, school. Please help me remember that you never change, and that you will always be there to support me. Thank you for that. Amen.

Devotion #84

"Strip yourselves of your former nature
[put off and discard your old unrenewed self]
which characterized your previous manner of life."
—Ephesians 4:22 (AMP)

Change Your Clothes!

Stop being the kind of person you were before you accepted Christ as your Savior. Your old lifestyle—the rebellious words and actions—should be a thing of the past. Like a piece of clothing that has shrunk, it doesn't fit who you are anymore.

Maybe you started drinking when you were twelve. It happened at a friend's slumber party when you and your friends snuck some beer from the family's refrigerator. Within six months, you were a heavy drinker. You paid older kids a lot of money to buy alcohol for you. When you accept Christ as your Savior at age sixteen, you're thrilled. However, you continue to drink and hang out with the same kids. Your joy about being saved doesn't last long, and you wonder why. The reason? You're a new person trying to live your old life. It doesn't work.

So how do you make the change from what you were to what you want to be? Step one: Discard your old manner of life. (See Ephesians 4:22.) Step two: "Be constantly renewed in the spirit of your mind [having a fresh mental and spiritual attitude]" (Ephesians 4:23 AMP). This renewing happens when you read and study God's Word and listen to good Bible teaching. It's vital! Step three: "Put on the new nature (the regenerate self) created in God's image, [God-like] in true righteousness and holiness" (Ephesians 4:24 AMP). You are a new creature since you were born again, and your life should reflect this. "Put on" that new life—and wear it proudly!

Did You Know ...

Paul, who was formerly called Saul, was a great example of a person discarding his old life and walking with God? He went from being a killer of Christians to one of the great missionaries in biblical times. (See Acts 22:1–15.)

More To Explore: Hebrews 12:1

Girl Talk:

How often do you read God's Word? How do you carve out time to study the Bible? If this area is lacking, start with two to three days a week and build from there.

God Talk:

Lord, I have accepted you as my Savior and want you to be first in my life. Day by day, give me the strength to be a new person. Thank you. Amen.

Devotion #85

"Haughty eyes, a proud heart,
and evil actions are all sin."
—Proverbs 21:4 (NLT)

Miss Know-It-All

A snob—someone with a haughty expression and a prideful heart—treats others in sinful ways. We think arrogant people are annoying, but the Bible calls their proud actions sinful. Looking down on someone—thinking more highly of yourself than you should—is wrong.

Makayla tried to like the girl who moved in next door, but she just couldn't. Very soon she grew tired of hearing about the girl's former (better) school, former (cuter) teacher, and former (cooler) friends. To Makayla, it seemed the new girl looked down on everything and everyone—including Makayla. When Makayla or her friends talked, the new girl tilted her head sideways and arched one eyebrow. She sniffed a lot and rolled her eyes. She was called Snooty Sara behind her back.

Before long, Makayla and her friends avoided the new girl. They were tired of the put-downs, her swaggering, the disdainful looks whenever they spoke. One day Sara bragged to the wrong person—their volleyball coach—about how great her former team was and how talented she was in particular. The coac̲_____ ̲__ ̲__ she told Sara that she used to live near Sara's _____wn. She'd coached in a neighboring town before taking her current job. Her old college roommate had actually coached Sara's former team—through one losing streak after another. Sara wilted in embarrassment as her lies crumbled. "Pride goes before destruction, a haughty spirit before a fall" (Proverbs 16:18 TNIV).

Don't look down on others. Think of people as equal—or even better—than yourself. Then pride won't creep in. Give snoot the boot!

Did You Know ...

there is coming a day when the "arrogance of all people will be brought low and human pride humbled" (Isaiah 2:17 TNIV)? "The Lord alone will be exalted in that day" (verse 17 TNIV).

GirL TaLk:

Do you know anyone who seems like a snob? How does it feel to be around her? Do you ever look down on others?

More To Explore: Luke 18:9–14

God TaLk:

Lord, sometimes I look down on others and feel I am better than they are. Please help me remember that the only perfect one is you. I don't want my pride to take over. Amen.

Fun FacToid

Do you have too much PRIDE?

Pompous
RidicuLousLy snooTy
Image is everyThing!
Despise
Ego

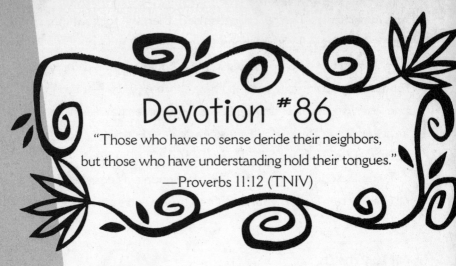

Devotion #86

"Those who have no sense deride their neighbors,
but those who have understanding hold their tongues."
—Proverbs 11:12 (TNIV)

Shhhh!

If you pick on and scorn people around you, you don't have good judgment. It's not wise to express negative opinions of others. A person with good sense will keep her negative opinions to herself.

You hate it when a new family moves into the apartment above yours. They slam doors going in and out, no matter how late it is. You guess they each weigh two hundred pounds—your bedroom window actually rattles when they stomp around. They yell over their booming stereo, and you now need earplugs to sleep. You complain to everyone in the building and urge two of them to call the police. Eventually your complaints get back to the new neighbors, and the wife visits you. "I heard what you said about us," she says. "I wish you'd come to us directly. We'll turn down the music and be quieter. I didn't know we were disturbing you." Embarrassed, you mutter, "Thank you," and close the door.

Try to live at peace with others. For one thing, not everyone will react as pleasantly as your upstairs neighbors. You could start a fight that lasts for months—or years. Gossip just stirs up trouble. "Don't talk too much, for it fosters sin. Be sensible and turn off the flow!" (Proverbs 10:19 NLT). If there's a problem, go peacefully to the person and express your concern. See if you can work out a solution together. You may avoid making an enemy—and gain a friend instead.

Did You Know ...

you can slip a note under your neighbor's door if you don't feel comfortable talking directly? If you live in an apartment, you can also ask management for advice.

More To Explore: 1 Samuel 10:27

Girl Talk:

How do you and your family get along with your neighbors? Is there an issue that needs to be resolved? How can you reach out to your neighbor?

God Talk:

Lord, I know no one is perfect, including me. Please help me remember to talk to the source of the problem instead of spreading stories and gossip. Amen.

Beauty 101

Even the most beautiful mouth is ugly if it's spewing gossip. Brighten your lips by keeping the kind words flowing!

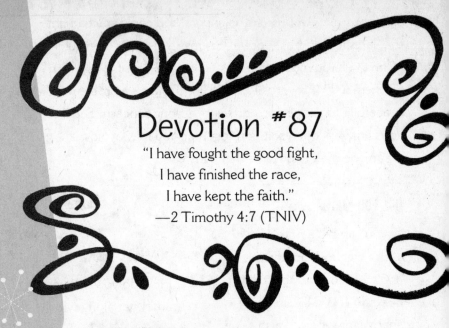

Devotion #87

"I have fought the good fight,
I have finished the race,
I have kept the faith."
—2 Timothy 4:7 (TNIV)

Crossing The Finish Line

When we get to the end of our lives on earth, we want to be able to say (like the apostle Paul) that we finished our life's race and were faithful to God along the way. Every person's life will be laid out on a different course, but we all need to overcome obstacles to remain faithful to God to the end. Starting the race is great—but finishing the race instead of quitting is critical.

Zoe accepted a summer job on her uncle's farm. He needed crews to detassle seed corn. Zoe was eager to begin. At thirteen, the only other summer job available was occasional babysitting. But working away from the city—out in the fresh country air—sounded heavenly. She could work on her tan while she earned money! However, Zoe soon learned that fieldwork under a blazing sun was hard work—harder than anything she'd ever done. Her arms ached from reaching overhead to pull tassles off the cornstalks. And forget the tan! She was covered from head to toe to avoid tiny cuts from the sharp corn leaves. She wanted to quit every time the alarm rang at 4:30 a.m. But she stuck it out, unlike half the crew who quit. In the end, she finished the job, drew her wages, and received a hefty bonus besides!

Life is full of starters, but how many actually finish? "My only aim is to finish the race and complete the task the Lord Jesus has given me" (Acts 20:24 TNIV). We must determine that we will finish our course—and finish strong. The prize is awarded only to those who cross the finish line. Every person's goal for the race is the same: knowing Jesus and remaining faithful to God. So run your race with determination. You can finish with joy!

Did You Know ...

the first marathon was run by a Greek? In 490 BC, Phidippides ran twenty-six miles to Athens, carrying news of a victory.

More To Explore: John 4:34

Girl Talk:

How is your race going? Is there any hurdle in your path blocking you from progress? Describe it. Ask God to help remove that hurdle.

God Talk:

Lord, I want to be strong and finish the race you've given me. Help me remember to come to you every day and get the energy I need to keep going. Thank you. Amen.

Devotion #88

"People may think all their ways are pure,
but motives are weighed by the Lord."
—Proverbs 16:2 (TNIV)

Why Did You Do That?

Most of us think we're doing the right things in our lives. We try hard to be good people. God looks at something else, though. He looks beneath our outward actions to the reasons for our actions. He looks at the thoughts and intents of our hearts.

You stop in to see the older lady next door several times a week. You feel you're showing God's love to Mrs. Jenkins and keeping her from being lonely. At each visit, Mrs. Jenkins gives you a Hershey bar or several chocolates from the box she keeps by the TV. If you sweep her porch or wash a few dishes, Mrs. Jenkins slips a five-dollar bill into your pocket. Your best friend even admits that you're nicer to the old lady than anyone else in the neighborhood. You don't tell anyone about the chocolates or the money, and you like to believe your only interest in the older woman is to be her friend. But sometimes you wonder—and feel guilty. If you're unsure about your motives, ask God about the situation. Only he can look into your heart and tell if you're befriending the older woman—or using her.

How can you tell if you have wrong motives? Study God's Word. The Holy Spirit will point things out to you, including your real reasons for doing things. "The word of God is full of living power. It is sharper than the sharpest knife, cutting deep into our innermost thoughts and desires. It exposes us for what we really are" (Hebrews 4:12 NLT). Do things for others—but for the right reasons.

Did You Know ...

Esther was a Jewish woman with the right motives? After becoming queen, she risked her life to save all the other Jews who lived in the land ruled by Xerxes. Read more in the book of Esther, chapters 3 through 8.

Girl Talk:

Think about the last nice thing you did for someone. What was your reason for doing it? Would God agree with your reason?

More To Explore: Proverbs 5:2; Jeremiah 17:10

God Talk:

Lord, I know I don't always have the best motives. I want to help others for the right reasons. Help me be honest with myself and you. Amen.

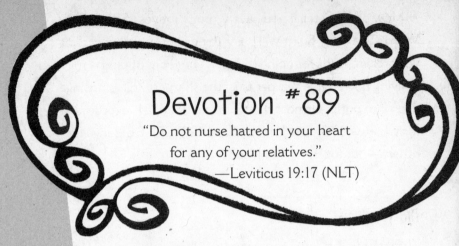

Devotion #89

"Do not nurse hatred in your heart
for any of your relatives."
—Leviticus 19:17 (NLT)

Be Heart Smart

Your relatives might do things that you hate. Even so, don't think about it all the time. The more you meditate on it—the more you replay the incidents in your mind—the more hate will grow.

Riley knew about hate, although she spoke politely when face-to-face with her grandmother. Her real feelings were another matter. "I just can't stand my grandma," she muttered to herself. "She's ruining my life!" she told her mom. "She makes me sick!" Riley told her best friend. Grandma had gambled away her savings, and then moved in with Riley's family. Riley had to give up her room to Grandma and crowd into her little sister's room. Grandma snapped at Riley about everything: her clothes, her friends, her music, her manners. She even complained that Riley's room was too hot in the afternoon for her nap.

"Then give me back my room and go home!" Riley yelled, finally snapping too. Riley—and her parents—were horrified at what she'd said. But Riley had been nursing hatred in her heart for Grandma for months. It was bound to come out.

"People with hate in their hearts may sound pleasant enough, but don't believe them. Though they pretend to be kind, their hearts are full of all kinds of evil. While their hatred may be concealed by trickery, it will finally come to light for all to see" (Proverbs 26:24–26 NLT).

What could Riley have done instead? What can you do if you have such negative feelings about someone? "When you stand praying, if you hold anything against anyone, forgive them, so that your Father in heaven may forgive you your sins" (Mark 11:25–26 TNIV).

Did You Know ...

especially annoying people will require constant forgiving? Peter must have known someone like that. See what he asked Jesus about forgiving such a person in Matthew 18:21–22.

More To Explore: 1 John 2:9

Girl Talk:

Do you have to hide your real feelings about someone close to you? Why is it necessary? Have you asked God to help you get rid of those awful feelings?

God Talk:

Lord, I'm having a really hard time with _____ right now. Please take away my anger and hate toward this person. Show me ways to be kind and keep those nasty feelings away. Thank you. Amen.

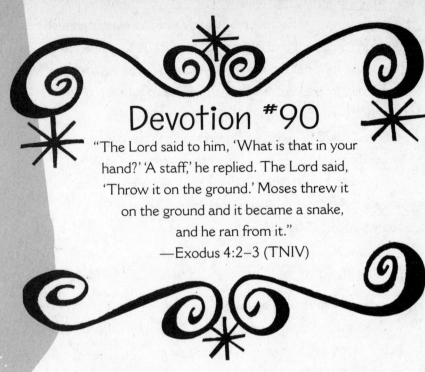

Devotion #90

"The Lord said to him, 'What is that in your hand?' 'A staff,' he replied. The Lord said, 'Throw it on the ground.' Moses threw it on the ground and it became a snake, and he ran from it."
—Exodus 4:2–3 (TNIV)

Snakes Alive!

God had told Moses to lead the Israelite slaves out of bondage in Egypt. Moses protested, saying no one would listen to him. God promised to be with him. God could use anything—even the shepherd's crook in his hand. When Moses threw it down, it turned into a snake! God could use the staff—or whatever was available—to accomplish his plan.

God also wants to accomplish things through you. In Sunday school, you hear about a "feeding the homeless" ministry in your city. You feel that God wants you to join this group. Even so, you're afraid. What will you find in the inner city? Will you be in danger? You have a decision to make.

After God spoke to Moses, what decision did Moses make? Obedience—

even when he was afraid. "Moses took his wife and sons, put them on a donkey and started back to Egypt. And he took the staff of God in his hand" (Exodus 4:20 TNIV). God is the same with us as he was with Moses. If he asks us to do something for him, we can count on him to supply the way to do it. "Where God guides, he provides." Moses' staff was later used by God to turn water into blood, bring hail and lightning, summon locusts, divide the Red Sea, and bring water out of rocks! If God can do that with nothing but a stick, imagine what he can do with you!

Did You Know ...

God used another staff to show a miracle as well? When Aaron's role as priest of the Israelites was questioned, God made his staff bud, blossom, and produce almonds overnight to show he was the right man for the job! (See Numbers 17:8.)

More To Explore: Exodus 4:10–17

Girl Talk:

Do you have any urges to do new things? Have you prayed about them? What do you think God is telling you? Follow his lead!

God Talk:

Lord, sometimes I feel afraid to try something, even though I think you want me to do it. Help me have courage and obey you. I know you can do anything. Amen.

Sophie Series
Written by Nancy Rue

Meet Sophie LaCroix, a creative soul who's destined to become a great film director someday. But many times her overactive imagination gets her in trouble!

Check out the other books in the series!

Book 1: Sophie's World
IBSN: 978-0-310-70756-1

Book 2: Sophie's Secret
ISBN: 978-0-310-70757-8

Book 3: Sophie Under Pressure
ISBN: 978-0-310-71840-6

Book 4: Sophie Steps Up
ISBN: 978-0-310-71841-3

Book 5: Sophie's First Dance
ISBN: 978-0-310-70760-8

Book 6: Sophie's Stormy Summer
ISBN: 978-0-310-70761-5

Book 7: Sophie's Friendship Fiasco
ISBN: 978-0-310-71842-0

Book 8: Sophie and the New Girl
ISBN: 978-0-310-71843-7

Book 9: Sophie Flakes Out
ISBN: 978-0-310-71024-0

Book 10: Sophie Loves Jimmy
ISBN: 978-0-310-71025-7

Book 11: Sophie's Drama
ISBN: 978-0-310-71844-4

Book 12: Sophie Gets Real
ISBN: 978-0-310-71845-1

Devotions

No Boys Allowed Devotions for Girls

Softcover • ISBN 9780310707189

This short, ninety-day devotional for girls ages 10 and up is written in an upbeat, lively, funny, and tween-friendly way, incorporating the graphic, fast-moving feel of a teen magazine.

Girlz Rock Devotions for You

Softcover • ISBN 9780310708995

In this ninety-day devotional, devotions like "Who Am I?" help pave the spiritual walk of life, and the "Girl Talk" feature poses questions that really bring each message home. No matter how bad things get, you can always count on God.

Chick Chat More Devotions for Girls

Softcover • ISBN 9780310711438

This ninety-day devotional brings the Bible right into your world and offers lots to learn and think about.

Shine On, Girl! Devotions to Keep You Sparkling

Softcover • ISBN 9780310711445

This ninety-day devotional will "totally" help teen girls connect with God, as well as learn his will for their lives.

Available now at your local bookstore!
Visit www.faithgirlz.com, it's the place for girls ages 9-12.

faiThGirLz!
the beauty of believing

Bibles

Every girl wants to know she's totally unique and special. This Bible says that with Faithgirlz! sparkle! Now girls can grow closer to God as they discover the journey of a lifetime, in their language, for their world.

The NIV Faithgirlz! Bible

Hardcover
ISBN 978-0-310-71581-8
Softcover
ISBN 978-0-310-71582-5

The NIV Faithgirlz! Bible

Italian Duo-Tone™
ISBN 978-0-310-71583-2

The NIV Faithgirlz! Backpack Bible

Periwinkle
Italian Duo-Tone™
ISBN 978-0-310-71012-7

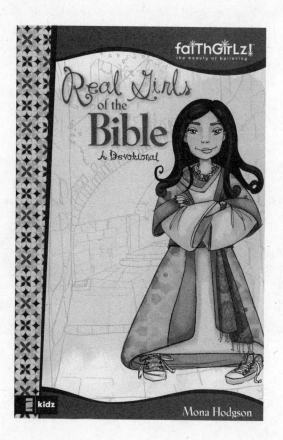

Real Girlz of the Bible: A Devotional
Softcover • ISBN 978-0-310-71338-8

This devotional includes stories of thirty authentic Bible women to illustrate the power of the girlfriend community to surround and support girls as they become real women of God, while emphasizing each girl's individuality and God's special plan for her.